Answering The Call
How I Took A Chance On Myself, And It Worked
(Kind Of)

By Rob Mooring

Table of Contents

*The names of most people have been changed for privacy reasons

Dedication

To my wife, who proved to me that true love is possible. And for teaching me that Bravo has some really good shows.

To my kids, who inspire me to be a better person. And for the screams and hugs every time I come home from work.

To my Mom, for her love and support. And for her encouragement when I suggested I get a Disneyland season pass.

To my sisters, for always giving me people to look up to and model my life after. And for always letting me crash on their furniture when I had nowhere else to go.

To my nieces and nephews, for giving me more joy than they will ever know. And for Kaleb and Delany, who truly convinced me that having kids of my own would be *so* worth it.

To my in-laws, both in Houston and Abilene, who accepted me from the minute they met me. And for loving my kids as much as they do.

To my friends, who helped me to like myself. And for allowing me to claim their families as my own.

To YCS, without which my best life doesn't exist. And for all the talent show dances.

To Dustin Peterson, who was crazy enough to think that these words mattered. And for predicting that I would call him from the car and say I couldn't write a book.

To Lindsey Thaler, who turned a pile of junk into a book. And for convincing me to work on it, even for five minutes a day.

To Lydia Smith, who tried to teach me what an antecedent is. And most importantly for not making fun of me for not knowing what an antecedent is.

Introduction

I call it the universal question: "What should I do with my life?"

It's universal because I haven't met a person yet who hasn't wondered where they fit in this world. Each of us ponders what we should do with the time we've been given. What's been perplexing to me is the lack of good answers.

Every once in a while, someone will say something smart about how to discover life's purpose or how to do work that really matters, but generally speaking we're left to figure it out ourselves. Some do figure it out, but most struggle. Many never find their way. In fact, according to a well-known study on engagement and satisfaction from the Gallup organization, more than 80% of people are actively disengaged in work and life, meaning that they intentionally leave the toilet seat up, don't refill the coffee pot, double park their car, or show up late and unprepared to meetings at work. They are actively discontent.

This is no way to live.

So how do you crack the code? How do you figure out your best-fit career and life and go after it?

I had a client the other day who said the same thing I've said before — "If I only knew WHAT I should pursue I'd go after it with everything I have. But I don't even know where to start!"

Enter Rob. I met Rob many years ago while we were both working at YES Prep Public Schools in Houston, Texas. Don't skip ahead, but you'll read more about how he got there toward the end of the book. Suffice to say, we're cut from the same cloth. We both believe that people can be happy doing what they love every day, but not without some soul-searching, sacrifice, and a little luck (in Rob's case, page after page of lucky breaks!).

Rob and I also don't believe in over-emphasizing the advice of others who know little about us and what we should do with our lives. We don't believe that money brings ultimate happiness. And we certainly don't buy the idea that finding where you fit in the world is an event, but rather a journey. This book is Rob's journey, but it's about any of us as well. I found myself in many of Rob's moments making all the same "mistakes." Like Rob, I also found my way out and into a vocation I love.

What I appreciate most about Rob is his authenticity — who he is today is who he was when I met him years ago. And he's the same person leading the sports cast for local news a decade ago in a Texas town. His story is all over these pages and his vulnerability is refreshing. But the real magic of this book is that it reveals a great truth of finding purpose in life; that is, there is no one path. There's not ONE way to get there. More importantly, there are no true missteps. Every step is part of the process, and each seemingly "wrong move" is a clue to guide you toward a life of more meaning.

Grab your highlighter, engage in the chapters, and take action on what Rob asks you to do. What you'll emerge with after reading his story is a clearer understanding of your own path. And, if you're like me, you'll walk away motivated to make a change, raise the bar, and contribute something greater to the world.

My dad once told me "there is always room at the top of any industry for those who love what they do." I've taken him at his word on that and believe it's true. And, assuming it's more than a nice proverb, I'm excited to see where you, Rob, and anyone else who pursues work they love ends up.

See you at the top.

Dustin Peterson
Founder and CEO of Proof Leadership Group
Author of RESET: How to Get Paid and Love What You Do
Career coach @ ThePurposeBlueprint.com

Chapter 1
I Was Part of the Problem

The most common questions I hear from high school students are the following:

How do I make sure I get into the right college and choose the right major?
What am I going to do with my life?
What if I want something different than my family and teachers expect?

These are heavy questions. Most students I meet carry the weight of expectations for greatness on their shoulders. They feel pressure from parents, loved ones, friends, teachers, and society to somehow ensure that they are "successful."

I worked for several years at a charter school called YES Prep. At my campus, over 90% of the students qualified for free or reduced lunch, and over 95% of our kids were first-generation college-bound students. I went home from work every single day feeling equally optimistic and sad. I was energized by working with kids that needed my help and could benefit from my expertise. But the circumstances and oppression that so many of our kids dealt with weighed heavily on my soul. Our students faced obstacles that I couldn't have ever fathomed until I met them.

Cynthia was one of those students. She was lucky enough to be born on U.S. soil, but her parents were not. Cynthia was the embodiment of all their hopes.

Cynthia was one of our best students. She was brilliant in every measurable way, and a joy to be around in every aspect. She was the type of kid that teachers, and her college counselor alike, would do anything for. And we all hoped that our own kids would turn out like her.

As a senior, Cynthia applied to the top schools in the country and got into a bunch of them. Because she was a citizen and her parents paid taxes regularly, she was eligible for financial aid. She was one of the lucky ones. Many of her classmates did not have that privilege.

Her financial aid packages were wonderful, making her dreams of attaining a four-year degree a reality. She enrolled at one of the best liberal arts schools in America. She graduated as our salutatorian, and I sobbed like a baby when she gave her speech at Awards Night.

Cynthia and I kept in touch throughout her college experience. The college she chose was located in the northern reaches of the US where it tends to be a bit chilly in the winter. It was certainly a change from Texas. I programmed Cynthia's new city into the weather app on my phone. I would call her when the temperature was below zero, which was often. And every time she picked up the phone, you would have thought she was going to school on a sunny beach. "Hey, Mooring," she would say. "It's cold but once you get below zero, you just stay inside. It gives me more time to read and study, so it's all good."

Not surprisingly, Cynthia was beloved on her college campus just as she had been in high school. During her senior year, she sent me a link to a video. It was she and another student doing a video tour of the campus for prospective students. She was a tour guide and had charmed everyone in the office of admissions. I am sure they all cried at her graduation from college just as I did at her graduation from high school.

Given all that, you can imagine why I was surprised when she texted me over winter break, asking if we could meet up. That in and of itself wasn't shocking, but the tone in her messages was. She wasn't the ray of optimism that usually defined her personality.

When she knocked on my door, the look on her face was alarming. She looked lost, confused, and sad. We exchanged pleasantries and caught up, but then our conversation took a serious turn. She started to cry.

"I don't know what to do, Mooring. I really don't."

Cynthia went on to describe the turmoil she was in. Remember how she was her family's hope? The golden child that was finally going to make it? She was five months from graduating college, and like any other kid about to finish school, reality was starting to set in. But Cynthia's reality was very different from mine.

Cynthia's parents saw college as a means to an end, a way to end a cycle of poverty. And neither of her parents went to college. Cynthia's parents thought that the easiest and most obvious way to be successful in life was to be one of three things: a doctor, a lawyer, or an engineer. They even told her that their expectation for her was that she earn more money than her father did. Because with a college degree, and a career path in one of those three industries, that should be easy. She could do that. No sweat.

The reason Cynthia was crying, though, was because she didn't want to be any of those things.

So as she sat on my couch, I realized that Cynthia was carrying the weight of the world on her shoulders. And I was part of the problem.

You see, Cynthia wasn't just the golden child in her family, she was one of the golden children of YES Prep. She was one success story that we could easily share to prove that our work was valuable. She could show the world that our academic programs produced students capable of getting into good colleges. She could show the world that I was a good college counselor because I helped her become "successful."

What a load of garbage that is.

Cynthia had checked every single box. She had gone to an elite school, gotten a great education, and was now set to forge her path down the road to success. And with it came a *mountain* of expectations from her family, her friends, and everyone that helped her along the way. She was supposed to *be* someone, but the problem was, she didn't want to be what everybody wanted her to be.

We had good intentions, of course. We all wanted the best for

Cynthia. But her impression of what that meant left her in a pretty terrible spot. She was under tremendous pressure to be a success as defined by everybody around her.

Once Cynthia gathered herself, I asked her a simple yet profound question.

"What do you want to do with your life?"

She told me that she wanted to be a teacher. She talked about how there were so many teachers in her life that impacted her. And that she wanted to do the same for kids like her. She wanted to apply for Teach for America, and work in underserved communities.

But she couldn't, she said.

She said she couldn't because what would she tell her parents? How could she justify the sacrifice made by everyone in her family to become *just* a teacher? How could she let everyone down?

Obviously, I started to cry.

I told Cynthia that I was proud of her. I told her that I would give my right arm for my kids to turn out to be *half* the person she was. And I told her something I had probably never told her before, but should have from the beginning. I told her that no matter what job she had, or how much money she made, I would be proud of her, as long as she stayed true to herself.

So we cried some more, and I almost outright demanded that she apply for Teach for America. And I told her that she needed to tell her parents.

I know Cynthia's parents, and they are wonderful people. They are the kind of parents you would take advice from. But they were scared, too. They were scared that if Cynthia became a teacher, and didn't ever become "rich", then why did she go to college at all? How was that a ticket to a better life? I didn't judge them for feeling that way, and I still don't. Being a parent is hard, and being an undocumented parent is even harder. But because I see college as a qualitative investment, and not a quantitative one, I had to disagree with them. Call me Pollyanna, call me a hippie, but I believe in the notion that you learn way more about being successful and true to yourself outside of the classroom than you ever do in it.

Cynthia called me a few months after our conversation, excited that she had submitted her application for TFA and had just had her first interview and sample teaching demonstration. She said she *knew* she killed the lesson plan, but didn't want to feel too good just in case she didn't get it.

Haven't we all felt that way? Haven't we all protected ourselves from disappointment instead of being thrilled at the chance of success?

I sent her the following text, and I share it with you now not to pat myself on the back. I'm sharing it because the thought behind the sentiment is a central theme of this book and how I see life:

Cynthia, going through life not getting your hopes up is no way to live at all. If you don't get this one, it just wasn't meant to be. I can't tell you how many jobs I lost out on that I was bummed about, only to be so thankful to not get those jobs in the long run.

It is okay to hope. Do it, as often as you can.

Of course, I could have used that advice myself as a high school student. And I think this book serves a purpose of telling you the things I wish I had known.

The bottom line is that if your gut is telling you something different than what everyone else is telling you, you need to take a moment to listen to it. Take a moment to evaluate whether your idea of success for yourself means something different than your parents', teachers', and other loved ones' ideas. And hope boldly, for crying out loud.

Remedial Biology Rules

But all that stuff is easier said than done, right?

I wasn't always what you'd call "driven." Certainly not like Cynthia. Some might have used the word slacker to describe me, and they were right. I earned decent grades in high school, but I wasn't the type of guy to go above and beyond in my academic pursuits.

I grew up in Houston. My mom stayed home with my two sisters and me. My dad was an undercover narcotics officer before I was born, and then did other things. They were kind of hippies. They didn't want me to spend too much time in classrooms if I didn't need to.

During my freshman year of high school, I took a Biology class. We took our first test, and much to everyone's surprise, I did well. The teacher called me up to the front of the class, and in a low whisper said, "What in the hell are you doing here?"

I replied, "I'm sorry?"

She said, "You just got a 98 on your test."

I replied, sheepishly yet sarcastically, "Should I have done better?"

She shook her head and said, "No. This is a remedial biology class. It's for kids with learning differences. Do you have one?"

Thinking I was on a hidden camera prank show, I said, "I don't think so?"

The teacher called the front office, and sure enough, I had been put in the wrong class. It was a simple clerical error. She asked if I could be moved to one of the other classes, but they were all full. Except the AP class.

My teacher then turned to me and explained that the simple solution would be for me to take AP Biology. She said that based on my grade I could handle it.

I immediately responded with, "Oh no, ma'am, that won't happen. My parents don't believe in AP classes."

It's true. My parents thought that AP classes were just standard classes dressed up with extra busy-work and projects. I think they also had a problem with AP classes being exclusionary in some way. I never asked them because what I took from their opinion was that I could work less and still be good. Music to my 15-year-old ears.

By now, my teacher was getting really ticked. She said, "What do you mean they don't believe in them? Like they don't exist? Like a unicorn or something?"

"No," I said. "They just think they are unnecessary."

She quasi-growled and told me to get my parents to sign a permission form for the switch because I was surely lying.

When I got home from school that afternoon, I told my mom that I scored 98% on my Bio test. She was moderately pleased although I knew she didn't really care if I got 98% or 68%. Then I said, "And my teacher wants me to be in AP--"

She cut me off before I even finished the sentence. "Nope. Not happening."

The next day, I showed the form to my teacher. She rolled her eyes and directed me to sit in the back of the class. I did for the rest of the year.

On top of that, when my parents realized I was taking credits I didn't need for graduation, they concocted a scheme to get me out of school on "work release" so I could come home at 11am. I took a nap and then watched *All My Children* with my mom every afternoon. It was the stuff dreams were made of.

The bar was not set high for me.

Which is why it makes very little sense that I was accepted to participate in Youth Citizenship Seminar (or YCS for short). It's a week-long leadership camp for outstanding rising high school seniors. The funny thing was, only part of those qualifications applied to me. I would have never qualified outright for a spot, but my Dad had spoken at the camp before, so they let me come. I was 17, and after the first day of being surrounded by 250 people who were better than me in every way, I liked myself even less than I did before I got there.

My group's leader was a guy named Kevin. He saw me walking to lunch by myself on the second day, and the conversation we had is something that I will never forget.

He said, "Why are you going to lunch by yourself?"

I lied, "Oh, I'm going to find some people I met yesterday at lunch and hang out with them."

It was obviously a dumb lie. He was my group leader, so he had been around me for most of the day. He knew I hadn't talked to a soul unless I had been forced to.

Kevin paused, looked up at the sky to gather his thoughts, took a breath and said, "You aren't a big fan of yourself, are you?"

My heart almost stopped. How did he know? Had I slipped up and accidentally put that on my application?

He continued, "There is this shell that you are in, and you've built it up over your entire life. And I know it feels so thick that you could never get out of it, but I am here to tell you that you can. I believe in you, and I wish you did, too."

Then he walked away. Almost in an instant. I'm sure I was sitting there with my mouth hanging open.

Talk about a shot to the heart. It was at that moment that I gave myself permission to like myself exactly the way I was. In that tiny moment, and in all of the countless others that I have used him for, Kevin taught me to dream and to be confident in who I am. I'd like to think that my love of people started at that very moment, because I finally loved myself. It was then that I realized that I had the ability to love other people, *and* myself, all at the same time.

I didn't realize I needed permission to dream. But I did. I wanted to like myself, to believe that my future could hold something wonderful. But for whatever reason, be it having low expectations at home or constantly comparing myself to people who were better at school than me, I just didn't believe it. I couldn't see what a slacker could possibly have to offer.

Moms are Annoyingly Right

In spite of that experience, I still tried to convince my mom that I shouldn't bother applying to college. I didn't think I'd get in. One moment of clarity during senior year isn't quite enough to repair a life-long career of academic underachieving.

To be honest, I didn't want to go. I was so deeply afraid of what it would mean if I got into college. First of all, I'd have to go, which would mean four more years of schoolwork. Then expectations would build. If I graduated, expectations would get bigger. If I just skipped the whole college thing, I could simply stay in the world of mediocrity that I had spent my life building. No change necessary. I could nestle in the sweet comfort of the known.

I was sitting in my room contemplating that sweet mediocrity one winter day when my mom knocked at the door.

"Hey, Rob. How are your college apps coming?" she asked.

"Just fine, Mom! I am working on them, slowly but steadily," I replied. Obviously I was not actually filling out applications.

After processing my words for a nanosecond, my mom knew I was lying. It's like a sixth sense for parents. I don't know how they do it, but they can read their kids like open books. She knew I was procrastinating because I didn't think I could get admitted. She knew I was too scared to even try. She didn't need to say that, though.

In the way that only my mom could, she just said, "You know, son, the odds of you getting accepted go up exponentially when you apply."

Well played, Mom. Well played.

I came up with a strategy to make her happy without really taking any personal risk. I decided that I would only apply to one place. I'd been to Pepperdine University several times for YCS, so I applied there. It seemed like a school with admissions standards that were likely to keep me out.

Satisfied with my own cleverness, I completed the application and settled in to wait for the liberating and inevitable rejection. I could say, "Well, Mom, I tried. It isn't my fault they didn't accept me. Guess I'll just have to find something to do other than college."

Probably due to a clerical error, I was accepted to Pepperdine.

Well played, Universe. Well played.

The Call

So what are you supposed to do with all this information?

Two things:

First, think about the expectations you find in your own life. What does your family expect? Your friends? Your teachers and coaches? Write all that down. Make a web diagram if that helps you. After you've written all that down, think about the expectations you have for yourself. What are they? Do they mirror what everyone else expects of you? When are they the same? When are they different?

Secondly, give yourself permission to hope and dream. Are there dreams you'd like to pursue that you're holding back from because you are afraid to risk trying? Are you letting other people's expectations serve as an excuse to put your own dreams on hold?

I don't judge you for doubting because there are plenty of times in the story you are about to read when I doubted everything I was doing. But know this. The only way to *really* know if it's the right or wrong thing, is to do the most terrifying thing. Try.

Chapter 2
Hold My Beer

My transition to college was less than smooth. Shocking, I know.

At orientation, I was hanging out with some people I had just met. They were fellow teenagers who were terrified about this next step in their lives. It was a dream come true for me. Having been on Pepperdine's campus several times (because of YCS), I knew the place well. At least I had that advantage over these bright, young students.

As a kid, I loved this set of stair railings by the library. They weren't shaped like the normal rails, you see. They had sort of a u-shape to them. If you turned to the side, it formed this perfect little seat, which optimized the combination of speed and gravity. It was like going down the slide, but obviously cooler.

I urged the group of ten or so of us to go check them out. The group complied, at best because they were nice, but more realistically because they felt sorry for me. But that was okay because I was about to show them an athletic feat that they had never seen before.

We have a joke in Texas, which is probably not the only place it's told, but it goes like this.

What's the start to every injury story in Texas?

It's, "Hey, hold my beer and watch this."

"Watch this!" I said to the group. I didn't have a beer, but the outcome was just as bad.

I perched on the stair railing and took off. Mid-way down I started to realize that my rate of speed was more than I expected. I hadn't done this since I was twelve, and I failed to compensate for my increase in height and weight. I started to wobble.

I wasn't worried though, because there was a landing between the end of the rail and the next set of steps. I'd say it was about 10 feet wide. If I could manage to land on my feet, everything would be fine. It would look like I planned it this way.

I landed on one foot. But not both of them.

I started to tumble, and I crashed headfirst into the railing. I scraped my legs and arms up pretty badly and probably sustained a minor concussion.

Everyone just stared in disbelief for the first minute. The first person to run down the stairs was a guy named Dave, who became one of my best friends. He thought I was funny and an idiot for trying such a stunt. He saw potential in that idiocy. He's a good man.

I dusted myself off, nursed my wounds (which involved wiping the blood off with my hands, and slapping them together because that, of course, gets rid of the germs), and headed to the next activity, which was some sort of speech/concert in the school amphitheater. Dave and I sat down next to each other, newly minted best buds. There were three people in the row in front of us.

Seating in the amphitheater was tight. I turned to my left to look at something, and before I knew it, the girl in front of me leaned back. Her shoulder rested on my still-bloody knee.

She leaned forward quickly and didn't turn around. Because that would make things awkward, right? Little did she know that behind her sat the champion of awkward, the guy who just invited ten strangers to watch him sustain bodily injury on the library steps.

I looked at Dave, he looked at me, and we looked at the girl's shoulder. There was blood on it. My blood.

Now take yourself back to when you were 18 years old. Imagine being the most awkward kid with members of the sex you are attracted to, and double it. That was me at 18. Don't believe me? Here is my senior yearbook photo:

What the fine folks at Harper Mills did for me was Photoshop all the acne from my face. All of it. The poor graphic design intern probably spent months on the project. It's probably framed in her house as her crowning achievement.

So imagine *that* kid, literally bleeding on the first girl he sits by in college. What would you have done? Hurried away with your head down? Cried? Fessed up?

I thought about all three in an instant. Dave and I had been friends for about ten minutes, but we had come to a deep understanding without even having to talk. It's like our minds melded together for that instant, and we both realized what had to be done. I had to face the music.

I tapped her on the shoulder and the exchange went like this:

"Uh…ma'am," I said, like I was her grandfather or something.

She turned, big smile on her face, "Yeah?"

"Um, well. I don't know how to really put this, but I just bled on you."

The look on her face could never be recreated. Not even the finest method actors in the land could reenact her expression. It was equal parts disbelief and abject horror.

"Are you serious?" she whispered.

"Yes ma'am," I replied, like she was the principal of my elementary school and I was in detention or something. "It's on your shoulder. Can I get you something to clean it with?"

She hurried away to take care of the problem herself.

Oddly enough, that girl and I became really close friends. Her name is Emily, and we ended up having a class together freshman year. We hung out all the time in group settings. She had an appreciation for my ability to memorize lyrics from rap music, namely Ludacris songs. She became one of the most influential people in my life at that time. She was a person I would lean on (pardon the terrible pun) for all kinds of things while I was in college. She even married one of my buddies and started a family in the Pacific Northwest. Funny how things work out sometimes.

The Gift of Gravity

There was something profound in my entry into college life. I tried something I thought would be awesome and literally fell on my face in front of a bunch of strangers. I got up, dusted myself off, and made a couple of good friends.

After my fall I thought my social life was over. After I bled on Emily, I thought it was unrecoverable. But in a strange way, I think that fall was the start of my social life at Pepperdine.

The first guy to come to my rescue was Dave.

It wasn't the only time he came to my aid. Because I slacked off so much in high school, my academic transition to college was brutal. I'll talk more about that later, but I resorted to shutting myself in my dorm room and trying to study the fear away. Dave finally came into my room and dragged me out. He taught me to have balance and confidence in my abilities. It has been such a valuable lesson ever since.

I probably took the fall for other kids who saw me, and who were nervous about college too. My vulnerability, however physically and socially painful it was, might have put them at ease. If they could see me bounce back from *that*, then their insecurities and inadequacies probably weren't so bad after all. Or at least it gave them something to talk about with all the new people they met that day.

The moral of this story, if you can believe it, is that it is worth it to try things. Even if the outcome is failure. Although I could perhaps have benefited from paying better attention in science class to inform my execution of the stunt, I'm actually okay with the outcome. It was through the vulnerability of that failure that I made two lifelong friends. And although I didn't realize it at the time, those friendships were among the most important things I'd take away from college.

I can't even count the number of students I've worked with who stop themselves from doing what they really want to do. Sometimes it is because they fear even the possibility of failure. Sometimes it is because they know their parents have other ideas (like Cynthia). I hope you will give yourself permission to take calculated risks. I'm not advocating for dangerous stunts, but rather, willingness to try things even if you aren't sure you'll succeed. And even more importantly than that, the willingness to have gratitude in the midst of struggle.

Your Résumé Looks Great, but Can You Cook?

One of my favorite students of all time ended up attending Pepperdine. His name is Jeff. It was such a cool moment for me because it was the combination of one of my favorite people and one of my favorite places. And being close to L.A. was perfect for

Jeff because his dream was to work for a professional sports team.

And he did everything right to make that happen. He made life-long relationships with his professors. His college resume was packed with things that a pro-sports team would love. He even interned for a team while in school.

But, like me, Jeff wanted to return to Texas after he graduated. He got an entry-level job quickly with a pro sports team. While it wasn't what he expected, he was grateful for the opportunity and worked hard.

He got paid nothing, so he took a second job waiting tables to make ends meet. And while he was waiting tables, Jeff's life got turned upside down.

The more time he spent working at the restaurant, the more he loved it. And the more he worked in his "dream" field, the more he realized that it wasn't what he really wanted to do. Jeff begged his manager to let him try every job at the restaurant. He worked as a waiter, a host, a bus boy, and in the kitchen. He was fascinated by the fast pace of restaurants and the ability to build relationships with your co-workers. So much so that he now wants to open up a place of his own.

Jeff could have easily said that working at a restaurant was beneath him in some way, as if a college degree elevates you to something more than you are. That's nonsense. And it's a dangerous way to look at opportunity.

It's nonsense because having a college degree doesn't mean you are better than anyone. And in my opinion, college is the place to find *yourself*, and not always your career. If you go into your college experience thinking that the only thing that is going to change about you is your job prospects, then you are missing the point entirely.

Jeff may have started the restaurant gig out of temporary necessity and with no intention of pursuing that line of work. And yet, when he engaged with the work, he found that it was a fit for him.

When you start a job, no matter how big or small, think about how the opportunity could change your life not only in the short term, but in the long term too.

I can't wait to eat at Jeff's restaurant one day, but even more than that, I am pumped to see that he found something that makes him happy. And guess what? That career has nothing to do with his major and college résumé. And that is perfectly fine.

So check your expectations. What do you think will happen after college? How much of that is truly within your control?

The Call

I bet you have a dream, maybe a couple. It could be dozens. But I want you to think about the one that feels the riskiest and write it at the top of a piece of paper. The one that makes you most afraid of failing or succeeding. It requires you to be the most vulnerable to change or personal growth.

Then I want you to make two columns. The first is risk. And the second one is reward. I want you to fill out the risk column first. I am willing to bet that it will be way longer than your reward column. It will probably take you far less time to think about the risks than it is about the reward, because humans are programmed to think about all the bad things that can happen instead of the good.

Once your two lists are done, evaluate the risk column. If the potential risk were to materialize, what would be the tangible impact on your life? Can you mitigate any of them? How would you bounce back from setbacks or failures?

Now evaluate the reward column. What rewards would you expect? Tangible? Intangible? Can you create a plan that creates a more likely path to the rewards?

Now find your nearest friend, hand him or her your proverbial beer and say, "Watch this!"

Certainly, I'm not advocating that everyone invite bodily harm with poorly thought-out decisions like my stair railing trick. What I am saying is that whether you want to or not, you've got to learn how to bounce back from failure. Even if you're bleeding a little. This is one of the most important lessons you'll ever learn. Life is unpredictable and, spoiler alert: you're not going to be great at everything on your first try. But if you can teach yourself to be great at dusting off and trying again, you'll be miles ahead.

Of course, I still hadn't internalized that pearl of wisdom at that point in my life. I would go on to fail many more times before the message sunk in. And that's where things got really interesting.

Chapter 3
Just Because You Are a Human Doesn't Mean
You Will Be Good at Humanities

My first year at Pepperdine was chaotic. Your first year of college probably will be chaotic, too. College at first feels like a summer camp that never ends. You are surrounded by thousands of people who have never met you and know very little about you. So you are constantly re-introducing yourself, and answering the same questions. "Where are you from?" "What's your major?" "Are you that guy that bled on Emily?"

In my first term, I decided to take some required classes. You know, start off with something easy so that I could get used to the college workload. One of the classes I picked was Humanities 111 with Dr. Sarah Sampson. How hard could *that* be? I am a human and lover of human things. I thought getting an A in the class would be easy.

I thought wrong.

My first clue was the class before our big mid-term. It was a three-hour class, at night, and it was lecture style. So Dr. Sampson would wax poetic about ancient art and architecture for 180 straight minutes.

With ten minutes left in the class before the mid-term, Dr. Sampson talked about what the test would look like. I remember sitting back in my chair as images of those innocuous multiple-choice tests from high school danced through my head. I could totally handle those.

I quickly learned that there were, in fact, other types of tests. Harder ones. Ones that required you to learn stuff and to be able to discuss it at length. Dr. Sampson said we needed to buy a blue book. I had no idea what that was. She said that we could find them at the bookstore, so that's all I really paid attention to. She then said that we were going to be given a list of 15 terms, and we were to define each of them and give historical context and examples of all of them. Next she gave us 10 potential essay topics and said that she would pick three at random for the test.

It seemed daunting at first, but I wasn't scared yet. Okay, maybe a little.

Then she said that in order to get an A, we would probably need to get close to using every page in our blue book, which was still a mythical object to me.

I thought to myself, "How hard could that be? The books can't be that big because everyone in our 60-person class would have to get one."

I rushed to the bookstore after class, and saw that blue books cost seventy-five cents. I was pumped. Until I opened the book.

There were 30 pages in it. Three. Zero. I was supposed to write 30 pages on something? I couldn't have even written 30 pages on the first season of "The O.C.", let alone Roman buttresses and Baroque art.

But I took a deep breath, reminded myself that I had taken hundreds of tests before, and walked in with confidence.

I made a 42.

Out of 100.

Up until that point, I had avoided failure as much as possible. I had taken every easy class in high school, I took no risks outside of school, and it led to this really comfortable life. Because if I excelled in school, then people would expect me to excel in other things as well.

As you can imagine, I was a pretty dejected 18-year-old.

Your Room is a Mess, and So Are You

I shuffled back to my dorm, ready to start packing my bags for my extradition back to Texas. Surely, the powers that be at Pepperdine University would be alerted of my test score, and I'd receive a written notification to leave immediately.

Thankfully, a guardian angel was waiting for me in the lobby of my dorm.

His name was Gerald, and he was one of the custodians that cleaned our dorm. He was an older man, I'd guess in his fifties. I remember seeing him sitting in the dorm lobby while he ate his lunch most days. He was small in stature, but large in impact. Gerald never finished high school, but all of his kids finished their undergraduate degrees in college. I had spoken to him a few times before this particular day. He had a way about him that made you feel at ease. I felt like I could tell him anything, and he would give me sage advice.

And on that fateful day, Gerald was there.

I am normally a happy person, so Gerald knew something was wrong the moment he saw me slumping through the door.

"What's wrong?" he asked.

I recounted the story of the failed mid-term and I ended with, "…and I just don't think I can cut it here. It's too hard, and I think I should go home."

Gerald was a happy-go-lucky guy, too, but his face turned sour.

He grabbed my shoulder, squeezed as hard as he could, and looked me dead in the eye.

He said, "Robert, don't ever, ever give up. The score on your test doesn't matter, but the way you respond to it does."

His message was short, but the impact was immediate. I burst into tears. He hugged me, assured me everything was going to be ok, and walked me to my room.

Gerald was right. I could choose a different response to failing this test. I didn't know what else to do but ask Dr. Sampson for help. I stopped by her office, and told her my name. It was a big class, so I didn't think she even knew it.

She immediately replied, "Ah yes. You didn't do so well on my test. You made a 42 right?"

HOW DID SHE KNOW?

I told her that I was worried about the test and how it might be a microcosm of a much bigger problem. I was worried that I didn't belong at Pepperdine. I didn't have what it took.

She sat me down, assured me it was going to be ok, and said that I needed to see her once a week for the rest of the semester. I did. She helped with my study habits and with my writing. And I earned an A in her class.

If it weren't for Gerald and the benevolence of Dr. Sampson, I honestly don't know what would have happened. Maybe I'd have bounced back on my own, but it sure helped to have someone there to encourage me.

Call it God, fate, destiny, or whatever, but Gerald was in that dorm lobby, at that time, for a reason.

And your Gerald is out there too. You just have to open your eyes to meet them. And most importantly, you have to be willing to be vulnerable enough to let people know how you are feeling. It's scary, but it could change the course of your life forever. I know it did for me.

What I learned from Gerald is that you need to be intentional about the people you allow to influence you.

What I learned from Dr. Sampson, aside from how to study, is that you're much more likely to get the help you need if you ask for it.

The Call

Now, it might strike you as odd that I'm starting out a book about college and living your best life with instructions about how to fail with style. I guess that's one way to look at it. But I'd like to offer this alternative: you will not be automatically good at everything you try. And you won't know what fits for you if you don't try things. Some things will come naturally, and others will feel like trying to put your shoes on the wrong feet. You have to try things to figure out which is which.

The people you surround yourself with and the attitude you choose to take toward failure will hugely influence your approach to life. Failure and disappointment are going to happen to you at some point or another.

Part of learning to bounce back from failure is sharing your vulnerability with people you trust. It's important to find people who validate your feelings and inspire you to remain confident.

Some important people in your life might consider you to be dramatic when you are vulnerable about your struggles. Others might just tell you what you want to hear.

The most influential people in your life should be the ones that accept you for who you are, faults and all, and those who take every chance they can to build you up. Surround yourself with people that make you feel like you are the only person who exists when you talk to them. Be around people who inspire you to be more than you thought you could, and who make you believe that you can do anything.

They also need to know you well enough to be able to call you on your BS. They need to be able to get you out of feeling self-doubt, and more importantly self-pity. They need to be able to both hug you when you're crying, and scold you when you're whining.

Make a list of those people. Then take out your phone and send each of them a text and let them know how much they mean to you.

Not that long ago, I sent a random text to my friend who I've known since elementary school. I don't know why I did it, but I sent him a text to let him know that I appreciated him as a friend. And since I had known him for such a long time, I expected a certain reply that I certainly didn't get.

He texted back, "Are you serious?"

He had *no idea* how much our friendship meant to me. None. And it was completely my fault.

After that interaction, my first thought was, what if he had gotten hit by a bus the day before? He would have never known how much of an impact he had on my life. And I would have never gotten the chance to tell him.

So don't wait. Send a text to five of your friends or family members right now. Tell them how much they mean to you and how much you value their opinion. You won't regret it. And it might just help you out of a jam.

Chapter 4
28 Cigarettes Later, I Had a Dream

One day I was walking through my dorm, and there was a sign on the bulletin board that read something like:

Do you like sports? Do you want to help write, edit, present, and produce a show about sports? Then come be a part of From The Cheap Seats!

It was the first time someone had asked me a set of questions that I knew all the answers to. I liked and wanted to do all of those things!

Below the questions was the contact information for a guy named Nathan, who was the Executive Producer of the show. I didn't know what that was, but it sounded super important. So I called him and practically begged him to be a part of it. I told him I knew nothing, but I was willing to sweep the floor of the studio to learn how to make a show.

First he told me to calm down, and then to meet him at a water polo game that Saturday. I pretended to know everything about water polo, but was surprised to not see any horses at the pool.

It was love at first, uninformed sight. I immediately took to the behind the scenes work of making entertainment. The editing, producing, and directing was all fascinating to me. The Executive Producer turned out to be a student like me, and I immediately dreamed of being like him one day. How could a college kid create a show?

Later in our college careers, my college buddy Jim, who is a genius on so many levels, got a scholarship to produce a television show for our campus station. Like all other Pepperdine students, we set out for the beach to mull over this important decision.

After about half an hour, Jim said, "What if we did a late night talk show that felt like Conan O'Brien's show? You could be the host. We would call it 'The Robby Mooring Show' and it would be great."

I wasn't so sure about me being the host, but we made the show anyway.

It was a blast. I loved the humor. I loved being on camera, but it wasn't something I could see myself doing in the long term. I preferred being creative behind a computer.

I also spent a semester directing the campus news program. I hated it. It was too buttoned up. Too serious. It wasn't a fit at all. Of course, I wouldn't have known that if I hadn't given it a chance. I kept on working away until I figured out what felt right to me.

Earthquakes and Grown Man Tears

I took a documentary film class my junior year. Our term project was called Legends of Television. We had to interview someone who was really famous in the world of television.

I was going to interview Al Michaels.

Al. Michaels.

My first *actual* memory as a child was watching the 1989 World Series with my dad. It was an all-Bay-Area world series. The Oakland A's and San Francisco Giants played, and, after the Astros, the A's were my favorite team.

For six straight years as a kid, I went as José Canseco for Halloween. He was one of my heroes. If you don't know how ironic that is, just Google him and you'll learn quickly.

My mom finally got fed up with me being the same thing for Halloween, so she told me I had to pick a different costume. So I got some fake blood, sprinkled it on my José Canseco jersey, and said I was "Evil José Canseco." She was not amused. But I was a sports fan, through and through.

The lead broadcaster for that World Series was Al Michaels. That was also the World Series that featured the Loma Prieta earthquake. I remember Al vividly. He was the voice of my memories for so long. Whether it was when he used to call baseball games, or his current work in football, or his iconic "Do You Believe in Miracles?" call, he is the voice of my sports fandom.

Getting to interview him was equal parts thrilling and terrifying. I had no idea where to begin preparing. Thankfully, my professor had my back. Or he just recognized that I needed some extra guidance.

You should also know that my professor was the late and great Don Ohlmeyer. Over the course of his career he won 16 Emmys along with a slew of other awards. He was kind of a big deal. He said that he wanted to meet with me before I did my interview. His exact words were, "Look, I have seen you in class, and I am worried that this is going to go badly."

Talk about a vote of confidence. I bristled at his lack of faith, but then I thought about what I wore to class each day. Jeans. A ratty t-shirt. And a John Deere Trucker hat. How he took me seriously at all is beyond me.

I will never forget the evening that Professor Ohlmeyer and I met. It was unlike any meeting I had ever had.

Mr. Ohlmeyer told me to meet him in the cafeteria in the communication building, and to bring my interview questions. I was there half an hour early, and he was there before I was. He was a true professional in every sense of the word.

He asked for my questions, looked at them for about 25 seconds, and then pulled a cigarette out of his shirt pocket. He offered a two-word command, "Follow me."

The next hour was a blur. He didn't stop talking and didn't stop smoking for all of sixty minutes. I tried to keep track of how many cigarettes he smoked, but I was too busy taking voracious notes, trying to soak in anything this television god had to offer me. He tore my questions apart, and it was the coolest experience of my life. It was like he was giving me the answers to the test before I took it. It felt like cheating. It felt like the interview was going to be too easy.

I didn't sleep a wink the night before. I spent hours memorizing every word of my questions. I added a bold keyword or phrase at the end of every question, so that I only needed a millisecond to look down at my notes to know exactly what I was going to ask Al.

The sun came up, and I started getting ready for the interview. I put on my suit, and realized amongst all my preparation, I hadn't thought of something very important.

I had no dress shoes. Not a single pair.

It was an hour before the interview, so there wasn't any time to shop. I turned to my roommate, and he let me borrow his.

His shoes were a size and a half smaller than mine.

I crammed my feet into those black penny loafers and limped my way into the building. Professor Ohlmeyer was waiting, and saw me waddle in like a wounded duck. I'll never forget what he did next.

He took a deep sigh, rubbed his eyes like I had given him a migraine, and said, "Well, let's see how this turns out."

I only remember three things from the interview. I wish I remembered more.

I remember Al walking into the studio, and it felt like the world stopped spinning. Ohlmeyer and Al were buddies, so they were greeting each other and making small talk. The rest of us were in stunned silence. I am sure I shook his hand and said hello, but I remember none of that.

I asked him questions for almost an hour and a half, but I only remember his response to one.

I asked him how good of a father he thought he was.

It wasn't on my script. It was a question that popped into my head because he talked about his family, and how much he loved them.

But I thought about his travel schedule, and I imagined being a good dad would be a tough thing to do in his line of work. So I asked him about how he would rate himself as a father.

He paused, gathered his thoughts, and with tears in his eyes, talked about how he thought he was a "decent" father, but he wished he had been around more to see school activities, pivotal moments, all of the things that makes raising kids special. It was such a touching moment for me because it was the first time that a hero of mine had felt...human. Like a real person. You could tell that he was really re-evaluating a lot of his life in that very moment.

The last thing I remember is what Don Ohlmeyer told me after everyone had left the studio. He told me to stick around because he wanted to talk to me.

I assumed it was my last time to ever work in television.

It was just the opposite. He told me that Al told him that I was one of the best interviewers he had ever worked with, and then Ohlmeyer did something I bet he didn't do very often. Not because of who he is as a person, but probably because of the cutthroat industry he had grown up in.

He apologized.

He said that he misjudged me, that he thought because I wore ratty clothes and looked unprofessional that I actually was. He said that he was impressed with my work and the work of our classmates that made the documentary, and he said he was proud of me.

I had never had a feeling like that in my entire life. People had given me compliments before, but it was for things I didn't care about. But this was different. The experience with Al Michaels lit a spark in me that I didn't know was there. It was then and there that I dreamed about my future for the very first time. Don Ohlmeyer, God rest his soul, in an instant, changed the course of my entire life.

From that point on, I knew I wanted to be a sportscaster. That was my dream.

The Call

A wise person once told me that you know more about yourself than the rest of the world combined, and you are the only person you are *never* going to leave.

Think about the power of that statement! There is no one on this planet who knows more about you than you. Not even your parents, your best friends, or your partner know as much as you do about the complexity of your personality and the depth of your character. That's why listening to your gut matters.

Up until that point, I hadn't really been motivated by anything. Then I had a life changing experience that put everything into perspective. I had feelings that I had *never* felt before, and everything about it seemed right, almost as if it was destined to happen.

I realize that not everyone will get a chance to spend time with a hero, or a celebrity for that matter, but if you haven't already, you will experience something that makes you see the world in a completely different way. And you will feel something that you might not have ever felt before.

That's what dreams feel like. They impact you in ways you couldn't imagine and motivate you to do things that you never thought you could do.

If you haven't had that moment yet, I bet it's coming, and it might happen sooner than you think. So be ready for it. Recognize it for what it is, and think about what it means. And think about it deeply.

It may have already happened to you, and for one reason or another, you didn't pursue the dream that arose from that moment. And I get it. That resistance to change, success, and failure has led to me taking multiple years to write these very words. But as I do, I realize that I am *this close* to finishing this book, and realizing another dream in my life. And I bet you are also closer than you think.

So find that gut feeling, and follow it. It's worth it.

Chapter 5
Terrell Suggs Owes Me Money

A few days after my life-changing interview with Al Michaels, Professor Ohlmeyer told me that his son Drew had started working at a new company. It was called the NFL Network, and they were looking for interns. Because of the success of the interview, he said that if I wanted to be an intern, it was done.

You could have told me that I had won the lottery, and I probably would have been less excited. I mean, it was the NFL!

ESPN runs these commercials called "This Is SportsCenter," and they are funny mostly because there are athletes in cubicles and mascots in elevators. The commercials are parodies of what ESPN was actually like.

And while there weren't mascots, those first few weeks at NFL Network felt like that. People were sitting amid piles and piles of boxes. Rich Eisen was carrying a box to his desk. Hall of Famer Jerome Bettis was there, just hanging out. For a sports nut, it was a wild experience.

My boss Holly called me into her office one day and handed me an NFL credit card. And at that point, that was the coolest thing I had ever seen in my whole life.

She gave me a task. She said, "I want you to go to Best Buy and pick up a PlayStation and the new Madden game."

I looked at her puzzled but elated and said, "Sounds great, but why?"

She replied, "Because I want you to set it up in the green room, and your main job will be to take athletes from their cars in the parking lot into the green room and play Madden with them. Can you handle that?"

Could I handle that??? Could I sit down next to professional athletes and play Madden?

I sheepishly replied, to hide my elation, "Yeah sure, I think I can handle that." So that's what I did. I did all sorts of strange things there. I made bags of free NFL Network stuff to give to players when they came for interviews. I picked up a Quizno's sandwich for Terrell Suggs, and he never paid me back. I used to sit with the editors and help them catch feeds of reports from Adam Schefter...before he was Adam Freakin' Schefter.

And I didn't mind any of it. I was in my element. It was a complete blast.

I also worked at a horse racing network called TVG. One of my dearest friends helped me get a job there, and it was an insane place to work. I had a little desk in the newsroom, and it was behind the set where they did the live broadcast. So whenever the anchors were on the air, we had to act normally, like nothing was going on, because viewers could see us behind the anchors. The sportscasters would talk, and then cut to a live feed of a race somewhere in the US.

And that's when all hell would break loose.

Everyone but me (because I was broke) was an avid horse racing gambler. While everyone was working they would place bets on these races. Once coverage shifted to the track, and you couldn't see or hear what was happening on set or in the newsroom, everyone would start screaming and cheering for a particular horse to win. Once the race was over, there would be about eight seconds before coverage came back to the studio for the anchors to analyze what had happened.

But people that lost money were *pissed*, so there was always this massive SHHHHH about three seconds after the race so that we wouldn't look like crazy people behind the anchors. It was a wild, crazy, and fun scene. I knew absolutely nothing about horse racing, but I loved the action, the live elements of television. It was thrilling.

You're From Texas So it Makes Perfect Sense

Even with all of these incredible experiences, I still avoided making post-graduation plans like the plague. I bet the NFL Network or TVG would have hired me if I had simply asked, even if it was just to make coffee or buy Quiznos for football players. I knew *what* I wanted to do, but I wasn't sure *where* I wanted to do it. And as anyone from Texas can tell you, this state is like a tractor beam. Once you fall in love with it, it's hard not to come home.

About a month before the end of school, I was sitting in my apartment drinking a mini Budweiser with my roommate. Our buddy Brad stopped by. His after-college plans were much more developed than mine.

"Dude, I am going to grad school in Texas. You should move with me. I mean since you are from there."

No details, not even a bullet point breakdown of a plan or reasons to go.

I said, "Texas is pretty big. Where in Texas?"

Brad replied, "Abilene."

If you ask anyone from Texas, or anyone that has a general knowledge of the Lone Star State, where in Texas you probably *shouldn't* live, it's Abilene. It's not like I had ever visited. This notion was mostly based on ignorance and fear of the unknown. I fell into the same trap that a lot of people fall into. We base our entire knowledge of a place, relationship, person, or group of people based on hearsay and third-party information. I had heard that Abilene was a terrible place, mostly from people who lived in huge cities, and couldn't see any value in a place that didn't have a million people and 12 shopping malls. And since I was a kid from a big city, I just believed them. No further information necessary. Thus, my immediate response.

"Hell, no."

But you see, Brad was the used car salesman of our friend group. And every friend group has one. It might be you, and you don't even know it. You are like a sleazy savant. Charming, friendly, but most of all, persuasive.

He came by it honestly. One time Brad and his dad were going to a Pepperdine basketball game. We were playing a rival, so our already small parking lot was packed with cars. Brad and his dad were late, so they hatched a plan.

They pulled into the parking lot that had a security guard. The guard said, "Can I help you?"

Brad's dad, without skipping a beat, said, "Hi. Nice to meet you. My name is Andy Benton, and I am just trying to get to my parking space."

Andy Benton was the President of Pepperdine. The guard clearly didn't know what the president looked like and also was afraid he was going to get fired, so he directed Brad and his dad to the Presidential parking spot. I still don't know where Andy Benton parked that night.

So Brad's response, which was incredibly profound in hindsight, was, "Dude just do it. You can move there with me, and we will figure it out."

I didn't know it then, but Brad had just told me the secret to life itself. The simple idea of taking a risk and seeing what happens seemed ludicrous at the time, but it's been a key to my success ever since.

At that point in my life, I wasn't exactly what you would call a planner. I was 22 years old, and I had never even owned a planner. I got through college by studying periodically and being friends with my professors. It wasn't fake; I genuinely liked them, and I think they helped me out because they liked me, too. To me, college boiled down to being present. I went to class as much as I could, aside from Disneyland trips and March Madness, and took professors up on their office hours. As a kid you think most adults are people who yell at you to get off of their lawn, but I found my professors to be fascinating people with fascinating personal lives. They were used to getting questions about their class, but not about *them*. So I got to know them because I was genuinely interested, and it wasn't because I wanted them to help me with my grade. And in the end, that probably helped my grade. I loved strangers, and genuinely still do, but as far as long-range plans, goal setting, and planning, that was not my style.

With all this in mind, the rationale of "dude, just do it" was all I needed. But it was still Abilene, so Brad and I agreed that I would look for a job all summer and if nothing came up, I would pack my bags for The Big Country (Abilene is actually called that).

The Call

I had a student a few years back that was stupid smart. I mean, just off the charts brilliant. She was the kind of kid that took every difficult class our school offered, and *never* made a B on a report card.

She said something in my office one day that I will never forget. She was telling me about a conversation that she had with her parents. She was on a competitive swim team, and she was struggling. She was one of the slowest on the team, so her parents asked her if she wanted to quit after the season was over and she had fulfilled her commitment to the team.

And she told them no, and that even though she wasn't doing well in swimming, she still found meaning in it. She still valued the journey she was on.

That kind of perspective in a young person is hard to come by at any age.

The craziest part of this story was that she had this conversation with her parents when she was *nine*.

There aren't many grown-ups with that kind of outlook on life, let alone a typical nine-year-old, but this kid was obviously far from typical.

So you could imagine my surprise when she walked into my office, and had the most serious look on her face I had ever seen from her.

She walked in, sat down, and sunk what looked like the weight of the world into a chair and said, "Mr. Mooring, I don't know what to do."

She then described her dilemma; she had gotten into two of *the* most selective schools in the country, and she didn't know where to go. One was closer to home, and one wasn't, and she was super close with her parents. She asked for my professional opinion, unaware that I had none, so I responded with, "You realize you are picking between a Maserati and a Ferrari right?" And I didn't want to discount her feelings, but she would be hard pressed to make a bad choice.

She made the choice on April 30th, and the deadline to make a choice is May 1st.

She enrolled on April 30th, and then I didn't see her on May 1st.

But I did on May 2nd. She burst into my office at 6:45 AM, sobbing uncontrollably. She broke down and said that she had made the wrong choice. She chose the school far from home, and should have chosen the one closer to home.

She was desperate, and told me she had already sent an email to the school she regretted not choosing to see if they had a spot available for her. They told her no, and she lost it. She told me that she was worried that she had made the biggest mistake of her life.

Although our paths were very different, my story and the student's story was essentially the same. We waited until the last minute, hoping that the world would tell us what to do. And when it didn't, we forced ourselves into a decision.

And the reason we waited was because we were reactive instead of proactive. And we were too anxious about what could go wrong, instead of making a decision, living with it, and figuring it out along the way. We were waiting for some miracle or sign to help us decide, when in all reality, we had the wherewithal to know what we should do.

So I moved to Abilene, and this student stayed at the school far from home. I got an email from her a few months ago, and she had been selected to this prestigious scholarship and research program, and is *in love* with the school she chose. It worked out, better than she could have imagined.

So now, I had a decision to make. And it was a biggie.

Chapter 6
My Entire Life in the Trunk of a Honda Civic

I finished up my classes, graduated, and moved in with my sister, Julie, in my hometown of Houston. I immediately got to work sending my résumé to potential employers. The ridiculous thing was that I had no earthly idea what I wanted to do with my life specifically. I wanted to work in a non-news environment, but because I was in Texas, I didn't think I had an outlet to do it. But I needed a job to, you know, pay for things, so I sent my résumé to every news station that had any kind of entry level opening. I probably sent my résumé to 20 or 30 places. I was applying for jobs that were normally given to high school kids. Most of them were part-time and minimum wage. At that point, minimum wage in Texas was a robust $5.15 an hour.

But I didn't care about the pay. I just wanted my foot in the door. Just an opportunity. A chance to get in, outwork everyone, and build a career.

A week passed.

Then two, and three.

A month and a half. Still nothing. Not a single reply.

At that point, I put my tail between my legs and flew to California for YCS, the camp I referred to earlier. By this time, I was working at the camp as a group leader. That's right, the kid who didn't like himself had now been given the chance to convince other kids that they should like themselves, too. Funny how the world works.

Given how influential and positive the camp had been in my life, I shouldn't have been surprised by what happened next.

My Nokia cell phone (which weighed approximately six kilos) began to ring on the second day of camp. It was from a number I didn't recognize. Courageously, I let it go to voicemail.

I forget the name of the lady who called me, so we will call her

Amy. Amy left me a voicemail that said, "Hello, Rob. This is Amy with KTXS in Abilene, TX. We received your résumé and I would love to talk to you about potentially coming in for an interview at our station. So give me a call back when you get a chance."

It was one of the weirdest moments of my life.

Of all the places I sent my résumé to, the only one to call me back was in Abilene? The exact place where Brad was going to go for grad school? What are the odds of that?

It was the second time I felt something *deep* in my gut. And I'm not talking about the gut feeling of which ice cream flavor felt right; it's the feeling you get that convinces you to take a risk, to go out on a limb and do something *big*. That's what it felt like. Full disclosure, I am a believer. I grew up in church, every Sunday, bright-eyed and bushy-tailed. But this was different. I wouldn't have attributed this call to God at the time, but looking back on it, I truly believe that there was a higher power pushing me towards something. This is what I needed to do.

Call it destiny. Call it providence. Call it complete coincidence if you want, but I know that call was a pivotal moment in my life, and I bet you'll get a call sooner than later, if you haven't already. The question is, are you going to answer it?

None of This Makes Sense, So Let's Do It Anyway

So I called Amy back and said, "Hey Amy, I actually don't live in Abilene, is that a problem?"

I actually said those words. Those exact words. She should have hung up on me, or at least laughed in my face.

Sounding a bit perplexed, she said, "Ooooh-kay. Well if you are ever in the area, let me know, and you can come in for an interview."

As soon as I got home, I told my sisters the good news. I was moving to Abilene in a week or two.

My sisters are some of the most wonderful people on planet Earth. They are kind, courteous, generous, and wonderful moms and wives. But the other thing they are is protective. They always treated me like their baby cub. They looked out for me and made my childhood relatively carefree, which was impressive because our life wasn't always that way.

So it's not their fault that they still saw me as the baby cub at 22 years old. I don't blame them. Here's what the conversation sounded like when I told my oldest sister I was moving.

"Hey Julie, I decided to move to Abilene."

"Texas?" she said.

"Yes."

"Why?" she replied.

"I don't know," I said.

"What do you mean you don't know?"

"Well, Brad is moving there, and I don't have anything else to do, so it feels like the right thing to do." Profound, I know.

Puzzled, she gathered herself and said, "Well, do you have a job?"

"No."

She followed up with, "A place to live?"

"No."

Finally, Julie said, in a way that only my sister can, "Well, you can always come back. Can I help you pack?"

My other sister, Amber, was similarly skeptical. Again, I don't blame her at all. Thus far, I had skated through life without real responsibility or foresight. But nevertheless, I was moving.

The Call

Case in point with a student from YES Prep, which was the school I mentioned in the first chapter. She wasn't one of my advisees, but the counselor who was assigned to her told me about her story as it was happening. Let's call her Anne. Anne was one of our best students and was applying to some heavy-hitter schools.

She was also applying to a school in town that was not very selective, but she only did that because her counselor told her she should. Being admitted to a four-year institution was a graduation requirement for our students, so the counselor advised her to apply to this school, get in, and then she wouldn't have to worry about that requirement any more.

Anne got into the less selective school, and she also got into the school that was *very* selective.

She had a choice to make, and to us, it wasn't a choice at all. The more selective school was "better" and certainly gave her more financial aid, so it seemed like a no brainer to us.

And then she picked the less selective school.

We were stunned. We thought, how could you pass up such an opportunity?

But luckily for Anne, and educationally for us, she knew herself better than any of us ever could.

After I switched jobs, Anne's story kind of slipped my mind. Every morning I read a higher education blog, and one day there was an ad in it from the university she decided to attend. The ad featured a scientist doing advanced research. It was Anne!

I clicked on the link, and it sent me to an article about two college professors that recruited students to help them with water bacteria research following Hurricane Harvey. And her picture was at the top of the article.

Talk about an absolute punch in the gut and a severe reality check for me. All of these years I told students that where they went to college mattered less than the actual *best fit* for them, but I wasn't following my own advice.

But this kid *knew* what she wanted, and the school she chose felt right. Anne went with her gut, and it was the best decision she ever made.

There are going to be times in your life where you make a decision, and you are the only person who thinks it's a good idea. Everyone else will try and talk you out of it while having the best intentions, but they don't know you like you know you.

So next time you have that gut feeling to do something, listen to that feeling, and go for it. Neuroscience is behind me. A 2018 study from the Duke School of Medicine acknowledged the anatomy and science of gut feelings, and how they can be powerful representations of your feelings and thoughts.

I moved to West Texas because my gut told me it was what I should do. It didn't make sense to anybody else, but that didn't matter. I knew it was the right choice for me.

Chapter 7
Dress for the Job You Won't Get

Up until I started packing my car to move, I was feeling pretty courageous. But once it got closer and closer to me leaving the wonderful, comfortable home that my sister was letting me crash in, I started to panic.

What on Earth was I doing?

Earlier in the day, I had called Amy from KTXS and told her I was moving to Abilene. I honestly thought that she would hang up the phone because they had filled the job, or she realized I was crazy for applying to a job in a city I didn't live close to.

It still shocks me that she didn't say, "Really? Are you sure?" I have no idea, but I am guessing Amy wasn't a mom. Any mom in her right mind would have tried to talk me out of it because clearly, I was making a mistake. She was offering a job that was part-time and paid $5.15 an hour. But Amy asked me to come in the next day at two o'clock, so I agreed. My guess is that she didn't care where the person who would fill the job came from. All she cared about was that it might be filled.

Back then, GPS wasn't a thing that was on everyone's cell phone. It was something only rich folks had in their cars, so I printed directions on MapQuest and set off for Abilene. MapQuest told me to go through Dallas. If you aren't familiar with Texas geography, it basically told me to drive a right angle, going North first, and then turning West. Apparently the algorithm for MapQuest didn't include the rule about shortest distances and straight lines.

Nine hours later (for what should have been a six-and-a-half-hour drive), I made it into the city limits of Abilene. I had 15 minutes until my interview was supposed to start. It was late July in Texas, the temperature was about a thousand degrees, and I was wearing my suit. Because what else does one wear to an interview for a minimum wage job?

I started to panic. This was my first *real* job interview. And I was late. Remember, smart phones weren't a thing at this time, either, so I couldn't just Google the number for the station and call to say I was late. I had to think of something. I decided to call Brad.

Brad and his dad were staying in town at a local motel. It's probably called a motel because they couldn't be honest in naming their establishment. If they were, it would have been called The Flea Bag. But remember, Brad is the used car salesman, always looking for the best deal.

I asked him to get the phone book from their room and look up the number to KTXS. Once I got the number, I called the lady at the front desk. I told her I was lost, and she seemed shocked. Abilene is not a large place, but I was 22, sweaty, scared out of my mind, and incapable of thinking clearly. She stayed on the phone with me until I got to the parking lot. I got my briefcase (a manila folder that held my résumé), hopped out of my 2001 Honda Civic, and walked to the front desk.

When I told them what I was there for, they looked at me like I was naked from head to toe. "You're interviewing for the production assistant job? Are you sure?" Bad sign. Horrible sign.

After a few minutes, they sent me back to Amy's office. She was out getting coffee, so I sat down in a chair across from her desk. After a few minutes, I heard her footsteps coming down the hallway. I thought, "This is it. This is the moment you see in the movies. This is the calm before I launch into a successful career in life. This is a moment I will remember as defining the rest of my entire future."

I stood up, put a smile on my face, straightened my suit, stuck out my hand, and then I saw Amy.

Amy was wearing a t-shirt that had a slinky on it.

"Nice suit," she said.

Slinkys Can Be Judgy

Where was the network executive with the three-piece suit that played hardball? I was always told to dress for the job you want, not the job you have. Amy invalidated that little pearl of wisdom immediately. I learned pretty quickly that in life, outside of the comfy bubble of college, there are no hard and fast rules. Was it a good idea to wear a suit to my interview? I thought so at the time. But it would have been a better idea to do my homework, understand the culture of the job I wanted, and try and find some sort of common ground. That's not just a lesson in wardrobe. That was a lesson in life I learned in an instant.

We talked for about 20 minutes, and Amy from KTXS told me that she couldn't offer me the job, not because she didn't want to hire me, but because she wasn't sure if the position was available yet. Someone was thinking about taking a promotion and hadn't decided. She said she would let me know in a week.

A promotion? What, from $5.15 an hour to $5.25? What was there to think about? How was this my life????

And by the way, did she not get the memo that I had a fancy degree in exactly the field necessary for this minimum wage job, and that she would be lucky to have me? And not the other way around?

I walked back to my car. It was an awfully long day filled with sweating, and I was on the verge of tears. This was not the way I envisioned the day going. Amy was supposed to be impressed with my credentials and my snazzy suit. She would note my many accomplishments and the way I had checked every box on the college student to-do list. She was supposed to offer me the job on the spot. Instead I had to wait a week to hear if I could get paid minimum wage? Talk about a punch in the face. Talk about adversity.

The Call

One of my favorite speakers, and a dear friend who endured more than everyone I have ever known combined, says, "Adversity is a terrible thing...to waste."

He's right. More right than I could have known at the time.

The last thing I could do was call my sisters or my mom and tell them that things were awful. I could never have called them and said, "You were right, this was probably not the best decision" for two reasons. One, then they would have been right, and I clearly couldn't acknowledge that. And two, I was embarrassed. Everything before that, at least in the areas of academics and good fortune, had come easy to me. I couldn't admit defeat. That would show weakness. So I drove to the motel, and shared a $49 a night room with Brad and his dad.

I know you're probably on the edge of your seat waiting to find out what happened next, but I'm going to pause here to talk about this for a second. Students have all kinds of expectations about how their decisions are going to turn out. And when things don't go according to plan, you find out a lot about the character of those students.

Before I started working with high school students, I actually was a college admissions counselor.

You read that right. The very school at which I bled on the first girl I met, actually paid *me* to recruit students to the school and make admissions decisions for students.

Any admissions rep at a college can tell you that reading season is a total grind. From December 1st until March 1st, I would read applications from 8 AM to 5 PM. Every single day. The work was hard, but I took it really seriously. I knew that kids' whole lives could change based on the decision I made for them. But even on my most generous day, I had to waitlist or deny seven out of 10 students. Seven.

Another part of my job was giving information sessions for students and their families that were visiting. I would speak for about 45 minutes and then answer questions. It was around mid-March, right after we sent out decisions.

As I was speaking to the crowd, I saw a young woman in the back of the room in the last row of seats. I assumed she was a student, just looking for a place to read or study. After I finished my presentation, some students and parents hung around to ask me some questions, and the young lady in the back row didn't move.

After everyone had left, and as I was gathering my things, she approached me. She stuck out her hand and said something that I will never forget.

"Hi Mr. Mooring, my name is Maggie, and you waitlisted me."

Uh oh. Big time uh oh.

Any admission counselor can tell you that this is an absolute nightmare scenario. I immediately began to panic and sweat because I thought for sure she was there to punch me or murder me.

I went back into the mental Rolodex and found the canned answer I gave everyone who got waitlisted. It's one that all admission reps use.

I began, "I am so sorry about your decision, but we have to make tough choices, and far too often we waitlist qualified…"

And then she stopped me, and said, "Oh, no. That's ok. I just wanted to come and say thank you for putting me on the waitlist."

I would have looked less surprised had she murdered me.

I replied, "You want to thank me for what now?"

She answered, "For waitlisting me. I have wanted to go to Pepperdine since I was a little kid, and I just wanted to tell you how grateful I was to know that my dream to go to Pepperdine is still alive."

I am sure I stared at her like she was a hologram or something. What I should have done was to be honest with her and tell her that the waitlist is more often than not just a soft no, or a stay of execution. But the more we talked, the more I realized what a terrible decision we had made. She was perfect for Pepperdine in just about every conceivable way.

I told her goodbye and that she would hear from us. I also told her that she should enroll somewhere else so that if we couldn't offer her a spot, she would have somewhere else to go.

She thanked me again, profusely, and then she left.

I walked into my boss's office, and I was angry. I practically burst through the door and proclaimed, "WE MADE A TERRIBLE MISTAKE! HOW COULD WE HAVE DONE THIS? I JUST MET THIS KID…"

My boss replied calmly, "Is her name Maggie?"

Apparently, Maggie had e-mailed and thanked numerous people in our office for her spot on the waitlist. It was the first time that anyone in our office could remember being thanked for such a thing.

Here was a kid who had a dream, and it essentially was blown up. She had worked for years and years to get the chance to spend four years at the school of her dreams, and we had essentially told her, probably not.

This may have happened to you when you were a kid, too, but when I was little, and I saw something I really wanted at the grocery store, I would beg my mom for it. And if the answer was no, but my mom didn't want me to throw a fit, she would say the classic line that all parents use. She would say, "We'll see."

"We'll see" is the equivalent to the waitlist. Is it possible that your mom remembers that Matchbox car you wanted at the grocery store, and will go get it for you later when the timing is better? It's possible, but the odds are less than slim, possibly none.

Is it possible that you apply to our school that everyone wants to go to, we tell you "we'll see," and then we remember you out of all the people we told that to and give you a spot? Possible, but I wouldn't hold your breath.

Maggie made a calculated risk by applying to Pepperdine at all. She knew the odds weren't in her favor. She knew how much it would hurt to not get in, especially when she had dreamed about it for most of her life. But she applied anyway.

Then she got waitlisted. It would have been easy for her to be angry, to dismiss it, and to hate us forever. She had every right to. But she didn't. She chose a different way to handle it, and she did it with grace and optimism. She thanked us, but in reality, we should have been thanking her for being mature beyond her years. She faced major adversity, and instead of seeing it as a roadblock, she saw it as an alternate route that could take her to where she wanted to go.

My boss agreed that we had made the wrong decision. But there was nothing we could do now. So we waited until May 1st to see who decided to spend the next four years at Pepperdine.

May 1st came, and went. And we were four kids short.

Guess who was the first person we called?

I wish we had recorded the phone call. She sobbed. Her parents sobbed. We sobbed harder than both combined.

Maggie spent the next four years at Pepperdine, grateful for every day.

The first thing you should know is that this is not typical. So please do not read this book and then go to the school that denied you and demand that they change their mind. It won't work 99.9% of the time, and it's not healthy.

But the lesson to be learned from Maggie is that the adversity you face in life can be the best thing that ever happened to you. I think far too often we think our road to success should look like this, because science says it's the quickest way:

────────────────────────────► Success

And science would be right. That is the quickest way, but is it the best way? Or the most likely way?

My path to success went something like this:

 Success

I think most people believe that the payoff of your journey throughout your life and career is success. And I don't believe that at all. I think it's part of it, but it's not the whole story. The things you learn on your crooked path to success are far more valuable than if you just walked the straight and narrow. The peaks and valleys of your path to success help you to learn more about yourself and the world around you than anything success can teach you. And those learning moments happen most often when you are in the valleys of life.

My challenge to you is to think of the last time you didn't get something that you wanted and felt you deserved. How did you respond? When, not if, that happens in the future, what kind of response do you hope to have?

I hope you respond like Maggie (I hope I do when I get told no, too). Maggie saw two things in her situation that were super important.

The first is that she saw the humanity in our decision. She understood that we had to make tough choices. She understood that we weren't trying to derail the lives of young people, but we still had to say no more often than yes. These weren't robots making these decisions. These were fellow human beings who were doing their best to perform what I can tell you is mostly a thankless job. No one calls and screams at you when they get in, only when they don't.

The second thing she saw was that there is so much to learn from not getting what you want. She was a fabulous kid, but clearly had been told no before. And that gave her the ability to handle adversity in a positive way, with an outlook of gratitude and optimism. Maggie learned a very adult lesson at a young age and handled it with grace. Now she works in a cutthroat industry and is thriving, probably because she learned how to get told no and still go after what she wants.

Maggie certainly learned, at a very young age, that adversity was a terrible thing to waste. I did, too, but it took me a little longer.

Chapter 8
How Much is $49 a Night for 31 Nights?

The next day Brad and I woke up, bright-eyed and bushy-tailed, ready to look for a place to live. It was a new day! Yesterday's setbacks would not define or defeat us!

We piled into Brad's dad's car and went to every apartment complex we could find. None of them had vacancies. We searched for hours and were turned away at every stop. We started to ask ourselves, why? Why did we keep hitting dead ends? We came to a conclusion that should have been discussed in the months leading up to our impulsive move to a foreign land.

There were no available apartments because Abilene is home to three universities, and it was August. Days before school was going to start. Of course there were no apartments. It would be like if I asked my wife to take a baby bump picture for our memory book, 10 minutes after she gave birth. That ship had sailed.

We started to drive back to the motel feeling significantly less optimistic than at the start of the day. Along the way, we passed by an apartment complex that we hadn't seen in the phonebook. The sign outside read "Eastern Oaks 1." My first thought was, where is Eastern Oaks 2? And why would they duplicate Eastern Oaks 1? It looks like it's a place where dreams go to die, and they decided to make two places like this?

By this point, we were desperate. We parked in the visitor space and walked into the office. The manager/landlord turned out to be a former Abilene city councilman. He purchased the property so that he could fix it up. While we chatted, we filled out applications.

It only took the manager a matter of minutes to scan the important parts of the applications. He turned to Brad and said, "You're a college student?"

Brad replied in the affirmative.

He frowned, "We can't rent to students." Then turned to me and said, "Are you a student?"

I replied in the negative.

"Great! Where do you work?" he said.

"Uh, I don't exactly have a job," I said, still feeling the sting of yesterday's rejection.

"Well, what do you mean?" he asked.

"I mean I don't have one. I had an interview yesterday, but I won't hear back until next week."

He looked puzzled. Kind of like the look my sisters had when I proposed the move to them. *You mean you're moving to a new place without a job? Or a graduate school to attend? Or a place to live? Or any plan at all?*

He said, "We can't rent this apartment to you, either. You need to have a job so that I can make sure you will pay the rent."

I looked at Brad, ashamed. He looked back, devastated. Brad's dad saw our despair, and tried to salvage the situation. He smiled and gestured toward the door. "Ok guys! Moving on!"

I started to calculate how much $49 a night times 31 days in a month was. Was it even possible to rent a motel room for that long? I had no idea.

Before we got to the door, the landlord said something that changed the entire course of my life. I often think about where I would be or what I would be doing had he not thought to ask one more question.

He said, "How do you two know each other again?"

We said that we were roommates at Pepperdine, our alma mater.

He said, "Pepperdine? Like the school in California?"

Again, we replied in the affirmative.

He looked down, looked up, down again, and around like he was scanning for surveillance equipment. Then he said, "Let's get you boys in an apartment. I think you (pointing to the unemployed failure) will figure it out."

We should have called Pepperdine and told them to change the admission view book slogan. "Come to Pepperdine, get a great education, and you too can be given access to an apartment you didn't deserve or qualify for!"

We were in. We had life. We had a chance.

I will never forget the first time my sister Julie and her husband came to visit our place. Remember, they are very protective, and were certainly at a different place in their lives than I was. They seemed visibly ill at the sight of my new abode. Not only was it a run-down place, but two 22-year-old bachelors were living in it, too. If we had hazmat suits available, I think they would have put them on.

But we loved that little place. We loved our neighbors. We loved hanging out together, kind of like college had never ended.

Where Did You Learn to Play Chess Again?

We were living on our own, in our own apartment, for the very first time. It was a magical time filled with magical people and experiences.

One night, at around 10:30, there was a really loud knock at the door. I was home alone because Brad was out studying. I froze. A scrawny kid alone late at night makes for an easy target. So I did the courageous thing.

Nothing.

I tried to breathe quietly so they would think no one was home. I thought I was in the clear, and then about ten seconds later, there was another loud knock at the door. I figured I could either let them in or get ambushed, so I went for the former.

I opened the door, and it was our neighbor Mark. Mark was about 6'3 with a muscular build. He was bald and wore mostly jeans and t-shirts. We had never said a word to each other before, despite living directly across from one another. Brad had asked him his name once, and relayed it to me.

I said, sheepishly, "Hey, you're Mark, right?"

His reply was a short grunt followed by a hoarse, "Want to come play chess?"

I'm a guy who loves to talk, but at that moment, I had nothing to say. The only thing I could think to mutter was, "Huh?"

I mean it was 10:30 at night. It was a Tuesday. Surely he didn't ask me to come play...

"Want to come play chess?" he repeated.

"Sure," I said.

If I thought that was weird, things were only about to get weirder.

He stepped away from our door, and pointed to his door across the hall. It was probably six feet from our door. It was as if he was saying, "Right this way to your inevitable death and demise."

"After you," I said politely.

"Uh uh," he responded, not all that politely.

So I went into his apartment, which was impeccably clean and really well decorated. It felt really welcoming, like your Mom's or your Grandmother's house. So naturally, it was at that point that I knew for sure that he was a serial killer. Certainly he was going to kill me and hide me for no one to find.

He pointed to a small table next to the kitchen, so I sat down. Was I making it too easy on him? He had said seven words to me, and now he was going to kill me. Should I be putting up a better fight than this? He didn't seem to sense my anxiety at all, which was not encouraging.

He disappeared into the back room for what seemed like ages. In my head, I envisioned him smiling into the mirror, looking over the different devices with which he could end my life. Sneering over the possibilities, whatever method he wanted to quench his thirst for blood.

I thought about making a run for it, but my legs felt frozen to the chair. The thought had barely crossed my mind again when Mark walked back into the room. He was carrying what looked to be a case for a chess board and pieces. But there was no way. It held some sort of blade, hook, or gun, I was sure of it.

He calmly sat down and opened the case as I shielded my eyes from the horror.

And then he placed the board on the table, set up the pieces on his end, and gave me my pieces to arrange.

One of the many problems in this situation is that I really didn't know how to play chess. And I certainly didn't know where the pieces were supposed to go. So I coolly tried to mirror his side of the board. Without even looking up, he reached across and grabbed one of the pieces, and moved it to its proper place. Once he was done with his side of the board, he got up and walked to the living room.

This was it. He was setting up the board to somehow make it look like an accident. Like two good ol' buddies were playing chess when something went horribly wrong.

And then, he turned on the music.

He had a huge, early 90's style stereo, and two three-foot-tall speakers, one on each side of the tower. If you are a teenager, ask your parents about this, but each tower had a glass covering that you pushed in to open and close. It made this weird, glass, springy sound whenever you opened and closed it.

Then, he turned on some slow jams. Google KC and JoJo and you'll get the genre. You know how in the movie *Home Alone*, the guys robbing Kevin McCallister's house always left the water on after they robbed someone, so that way the house would flood, and they had the nickname The Wet Bandits? I thought this was a similar MO. This guy murdered people in the same way, every time. Like some criminal mastermind.

I closed my eyes as he stepped closer to the table. Instead of stabbing me in the back, Mark just walked to his chair, sat down, and proceeded to *crush* me at chess. He absolutely wiped the floor with me.

After about 15 minutes, he had beaten me. So we reset the board, and then, another 15 minutes later, he crushed me again.

After game two, I got up the nerve to speak. Not a single word had been said prior to this, "Hey Mark, how did you get so good at chess?"

"Prison," he responded.

He didn't say another word after that.

After game three, with a similar outcome, he packed up the board, put it away in the back of his apartment, opened his door, and pointed to my door. I walked back to our apartment, and he shut his door.

We never played chess again. But Brad did. He met Mark through chess in a similar way. And every time we saw Mark around our apartment, we waved. And he waved back. The legend of Mark, and his fondness for chess, only grew with time. Mark also would walk around our building a lot. We never knew why, but we think that he did it to look after everyone. We think he did it to make everyone feel safer. And that was a comforting feeling.

And although having Mark around was comforting, nothing was really normal about our situation in Abilene. We never could have predicted the things that were happening to us in the moment, and what would happen in the future.

It wasn't always easy, but we wouldn't trade our experience for the world. So the life we thought we *deserved* wasn't what we were given, and it was the best thing that ever happened to us. It provided stories about the people and places we were experiencing that we will tell our grandkids about one day. It defined a turbulent, yet memorable and enjoyable, era of our lives.

The Call

I have found that the best way in life to be constantly disappointed is to feel like you constantly deserve better. I know that sounds self-righteous, because as we were moving into that apartment I certainly felt like I deserved at least a little bit better than this.

When you graduate from college, you may get a job opportunity that seems perfect for you, but little things will get in your way and make you decide not to take it. It might be where it is or the fact that it's not near a big city.

I hear these same reasons reiterated by kids when I try to put colleges on their list that they haven't heard of. I think that's mostly because their parents want them to go to a school people have heard of because it will provide a better "value" or "bang for their buck."

I had a family come into my office one time and they flat out told me, "We want our daughter to go to a name brand engineering school."

This is one of those moments a college counselor dreams of. I had the perfect answer in my hip pocket, ready to go.

I replied, "Great, have you heard of a school called Harvey Mudd College?"

They looked puzzled and told me that they had never heard of it.

To anyone in the college admissions world, Harvey Mudd isn't just a great engineering school, it's *the* engineering school. I went to a presentation on campus once, and they had students who were freshman working on projects that most adult engineers never had access to.

But these parents grew up in Texas, which can be a myopic place. So the engineering schools they considered "name brand" didn't include a tiny one in southern California. So much of our knowledge of what is good and valuable comes from our own experiences. But guess what. None of us have experienced *everything*, so we don't know what's best. Instead we rely on other "experts" to tell us what is best, but that expert has probably never met you, and doesn't know what's best for *you*.

You are the only person who knows what is best for you. Whether it's picking a college, finding a place to live, or finding a career field, there will be plenty of well-intentioned people that are going to tell you what's best for you. Accept their feedback graciously, and then trust your gut in the end.

I think about Mark and all the people I've met that have had an impact on my life. If I had discounted my job or that apartment because it wasn't "good" enough, then so many things I value in life would have never existed.

It wasn't all perfect, though. Looking back on that experience, I am honestly pretty conflicted about it. How many people had come to that complex before us, looking for a place to live, and been turned down? It may have been none, but it could have been many. I didn't realize it at the time, but I was given an advantage I didn't deserve. Was it because I had a college education? Was it because we were nice? Or at least looked nice? And what does looking nice mean? I can only conclude that it was a product of privilege, although I didn't recognize it at the time.

And while I was conflicted about getting the break, we certainly were appreciative of it. We could have reacted to the apartment working out in one of two ways. First, we could have been thankful for a brief period of time, and then realized that we weren't really getting a "break" at all. The landlord was giving us access to a crappy apartment. It's not like he was handing us the keys to Buckingham Palace. We could have gone on our merry, little, entitled way, but I am so glad that we didn't.

Instead, we were really pumped about that apartment. Aside from the fact that we wouldn't have to live at the motel anymore, we were excited to have a place of our own. We were looking forward to getting to spend time with each other and embark on the next phase of life. I mean, that's better than living with a stranger.

My challenge to you is to consider your own sense of privilege and entitlement. And there are so many different kinds of privilege. The one (of many) that I was dealing with in this instance was the college educated privilege. I think so many of us think we deserve opportunities to be handed to us because we have a college degree. And when I say opportunity, I don't mean the opportunity of deserving a living wage. That should be for everyone to have access to.

I mean the entitlement of thinking you are a big shot because you went to a fancy school and got a fancy degree.

One of the biggest problems I face when helping students with their college application and selection process is that they think the prestige or notoriety of the college they go to, and what they major in, are *the* most important parts of the decision process. They focus on rankings rather than fit, and that can often lead to being pretty miserable in college when you should be having fun.

And I understand the whole thought of having a college degree makes you qualified to do the work you learned about in school. Trust me, I had the same feeling. I was applying for jobs they gave to high school kids, so I thought I was a shoo-in to get hired. And it was a tough reality to face when I realized I wasn't.

I think I had that feeling because I was stuck in a mindset of thinking I was deserving because I could *do* the work. I had all of the skills necessary to be a functioning employee. And until I had to hire people myself at a job, I realized that logic is flawed in so many ways.

I learned that your ability to do the job is *way* less important than *how* you do the job.

If you are rubbing your eyes in confusion, just give me a minute.

When I was on a hiring team, we would get dozens and dozens of qualified applicants. We had lots of people with the proper training and job experience. But those two things weren't the primary factors in our decision process.

I heard a billionaire speak one time. When he was done, a person in the crowd asked him what he looked for in an applicant that wanted to work at his company. His response was something I will never forget.

He said, "I couldn't care less about two things. Where you went to college, and what your GPA was. Couldn't care less."

He continued, "What I do care about, is are you self-aware? Can you write? And can you work with other people? If you can do those things, we can teach you the rest."

When I first heard that, I didn't think much of it. But when I started the hiring process, it's really all I thought about.

Our decisions at my old job came down to three things...whether or not the candidates were self-aware, whether or not they could work well with other people, and whether or not we thought we could stand them for nine hours a day.

It was as simple as that. So when you go to college, or when you start in the workforce, it's easy to think about how important it is to make good grades or learn your craft. But what I think is vastly more important is to develop your interpersonal skills, work on being able to accept feedback and meet as many different people as you can. When you get into the workforce, you are going to meet people that have personalities or traits that you have never dealt with before. That can be really challenging, especially if you have only been around people that think and act the way you do.

There are going to be two questions at a job interview that might stump you the most. The first is, tell me a little bit about yourself? And the second is, what is something you need to work on or improve in your professional life?

I think the answer to those questions are the most important in the interview, and they are the hardest to answer. So instead of blowing off the first one and doing a humble brag for the second, think deeply about both of those questions. Spend time in college or your professional life trying to develop yourself in a way that you can answer those questions easily and honestly. I truly believe that I have gotten jobs not based on my résumé or experience, but on how I answered those questions.

So if you learn more about yourself in college than you do about your future profession, then in my opinion, you did college correctly.

Chapter 9
How Do You Spell Futon Again?

Brad's dad paid our deposit. It was $50. That could have been a million dollars, and that wouldn't have mattered to me. I didn't have $50 of disposable income. I don't know that I thanked Brad's dad sufficiently.

It was time to move in. Everything I owned was in the trunk and back seat of my little Honda. My entire existence fit into about three cubic feet of space. We took the key, opened the door, and entered into adulthood.

Remember Emily, the kind soul I bled on at college orientation? She was going to graduate school in Abilene, too. Of course, she was way more organized than Brad and I, so she already had a place to live. When we moved into our place, Emily came to help us get settled.

Emily decided to clean out the fridge and freezer. She immediately regretted choosing that job. The previous tenant had neglected to empty the fridge and it now housed seriously decayed food, complete with maggots. She never said it, but she must have been thinking, "YOU CAN'T LIVE HERE. IT'S GROSS AND POSSIBLY A BIOHAZARD." But she soldiered on. She was courageous. God bless her for it.

One of the first things we did was call the electric company. It was West Texas, it was August, and it was about a thousand degrees. It would have been hard for me to find a job if I died from heat stroke, so getting the air turned on was a top priority.

The electric company told us that it would take approximately eight days to get our electricity, and therefore air-conditioning, turned on. Eight days. Just like every full apartment complex we visited, their staff told us, "There are three universities in town. We are backed up with kids moving into apartments and needing electricity." Great. I was being judged for my lack of forethought again, and I couldn't find respite from the oppressive heat in my own home.

I finally called my mom. I didn't know what else to do. She said calmly, in a way that only my mom could, "You won't survive eight days, dear. You need to find another place to stay."

Fabulous.

As soon as I hung up the phone, before I could even ask, Emily said, "We have a foldout couch at our house! You can stay there!"

God is good. And Emily, too. We spent the next eight days on Emily's fold out couch. Me and Brad. Getting closer than we had ever been or wanted to be. Emily's poor roommates put up with us for that long out of the goodness of their hearts.

Meanwhile, during those eight days on a spring heavy mattress, I waited for that phone call from KTXS.

Eight days passed, and I hadn't heard back.

DOES THAT LEG HAVE AN "L" STICKER ON IT!?!?!?!?

On the ninth day, we did what any red-blooded American bachelors would do. Instead of focusing on the things we couldn't control, like when the power got turned on, we decided to turn our attention to something we could control.

We bought a cheap futon to put in the living room of our apartment.

And clearly, the futon is the key to the romantic success of any young adult.

We went to the Walmart down the street from our apartment. The place was packed from wall to wall with rabid shoppers. An employee told us that the store would be moving to a new location, so a lot of merchandise was on sale. That, combined with college move-in, was a recipe for unimaginable crowds. We survived the melee long enough to get the futon we had come for. In spite of the lack of air conditioning and electricity, we took it back to our apartment to assemble. It shouldn't take that long, we thought.

How naive we were.

We put the back of the futon together with no problem. When we tried to put the legs on, it became clear that something was amiss. This box was packed with two left legs and no right. It was a minor setback, really. So we took the futon apart, put it back in the box, and went back to Walmart.

They were nice, but busy, and told us to go get a new box. We did. We took it back to our apartment feeling relieved that the exchange went so easily. We put the back of the futon together with no problem. And then we tried to put on the legs. This time there were two right legs and no left.

I kid you not.

We took it apart, put it back in the box, and returned to Walmart. Again.

They graciously and apologetically gave us a third box. I know what you are probably thinking. Yes, we opened the box in the Walmart to make sure it had the right, or should I say correct, legs this time.

This process, which could have easily taken an hour if everything went right, was going on for nine hours now. By the time we got back to our place again, we were sweating profusely. And we were hangry. We went from optimistic to pissed midway between trips one and two to Walmart. Trip three was just irritating. You could feel (and smell) the tension in the room.

I know I kind of gave Brad a hard time about being the used car salesman of our friend group. But that same person typically is the one to get you out of a jam when you really need it. Brad is definitely that guy.

He looked at me, sensing our collective anger, and said, "Hey, do you know what the first two letters in the word futon are? F.U."

We totally lost it. Call it heat stroke, disillusionment, fatigue, whatever, but we couldn't stop laughing. I'll never forget that moment.

At that point in my excursion to Abilene, I was about ready to snap. I was jobless, we had no electricity in our apartment, and wrestling a futon was the straw that broke the camel's back. I was ready to move back to my sister's place that very minute. It didn't feel like it at the time, but that conversation, that joke Brad made, was a defining moment in my life. After that very instant, my life was completely different.

Brad and I were in this adventure together. He never said anything, probably because he knew I was really struggling, but this situation probably wasn't easy for him either. He was starting an intense graduate program in a place he had never been to, and we couldn't put the dadgum futon together. Yet, just like the influential people in your life (the "Gerald's" you will hopefully have or meet), he said the thing I needed to hear the most. If he hadn't, I honestly believe that I wouldn't be typing these words right now. My life, my family, my career, and my joy would not be what they are today. If I had left Abilene in the midst of the bad parts, I wouldn't have experienced all the good stuff I can see in my life today.

An Island of Misfit Toy

The most impressive student I ever met was also one of the most frightened.

I was spending my summer as a counselor at the Youth Citizenship Seminar that you read about earlier. She was about to be a junior in high school, and she had already done some incredible things.

She started a non-profit, a legit $501(c)(3)$ organization that helped provide educational equality to students in South America. She spoke at a TEDx conference when she was in high school. She was incredibly accomplished for someone so young. And yet, as I observed her interactions with other students in our group, I could see that she struggled.

A couple of days into the seminar, I pulled her aside to talk.

"I'm going to tell you something. You don't have to respond. I just want you to think about it."

She looked dubious, but nodded.

"No matter how much success you have, and no matter how many wonderful things you do, no one is an island. No one can do it alone."

Her face dropped. I could see that I'd hit a nerve. She just nodded again and said she'd think about it. I left her to it.

At the closing banquet, we all hugged, cried, and said our goodbyes. She gave me a note and told me to read it on my way home.

Her note said that she was moved by what I told her because she had spent most of her life being too proud to ask for help. How could the wunderkind that started a charity and spoke in front of thousands of people be vulnerable? How could she ask for help?

Have you ever felt that way? Of course you have. It's human nature.

And yet, falling into this trap is debilitating and limiting. Being able to lean on friends is such an important aspect of your potential success. Asking for help is scary because it makes you vulnerable. But without vulnerability and risk and help from others, profound growth is impossible.

The Call

I learned a lot about friendship from Charles B. Runnels, or Chancellor Runnels as I knew him. He's the guy who started the Youth Citizenship Seminar that means so much to me.

By the end of his life, Chancellor Runnels' résumé was fuller than mine will ever be, but that's not what made him a hero to me. What I remember most about him was his ability to develop meaningful relationships with people. He was great at making, and more importantly, keeping friends.

I remember showing Chancellor Runnels a picture of my wife before we were married. I told him that the picture was of my girlfriend. He paused, looked at me, then back at the picture, and said, "She's beautiful. So what's she doing with you?"

Everyone thought he was their best friend, me included. He probably had a hundred thousand best friends. He genuinely cared about people, no matter where they came from. He didn't make friends with people because of what they could do for him. I think he honestly just loved human beings.

I have tried to emulate that in my life too. I love strangers. It's weird. You put me in a room full of people I have never met, and that's a day in paradise for me. I get that from Chancellor Runnels, and also my mom.

When we went out to eat as kids, the waiter would come to our table and say something like, "Hi, my name is Bill, and I will be taking care of you this evening." My sisters and I would collectively groan because we knew what was coming next.

My mom, without skipping a beat, would say, "Hello, Bill! My name is Margaret, and these are my kids and husband," and she would give Bill all of our names. The waiter was always flabbergasted. Every. Single. Time. But they were always warm to us when my mom did that. It was embarrassing at the time, but that practice taught me to see and treat service workers like actual human beings.

I try to be a great friend to people because I have had so many wonderful friends in my life. It sounds cheesy, but it's true. When you put good out into the world, even the very small amount that I feel like I contribute, it comes back to you tenfold. I can't tell you how many times friends like Emily have helped me out of a jam. And I can't urge you strongly enough to surround yourself with people who uplift you, who inspire you to be a better person. And treat them well. Chancellor Runnels taught me that friends are a more precious commodity than all the gold and silver in the universe.

Chancellor Runnels had a *million* friends; everyone I ever heard him talk to was called friend. But he had this way of making you feel like you were the only friend that actually mattered, in that given moment. It made you feel important and special.

You could be like Chancellor Runnels and have a million friends, or you could have two. It doesn't matter. What does matter is the way you treat them and the goodness you put out into the world when you do. They will help you out of plenty of jams, and then you get to repay the debt. There is no better feeling than that.

I heard an idea about leadership that I found to be really remarkable. It came from the guy who convinced me to write this book, and he said that there are two types of leaders in this world: keepers and sharers.

The leaders that are keepers save the good stuff for themselves, so that they always shine. The keepers in my life have had a profound insecurity that they are dealing with from the baggage in their life, so they are afraid to be a sharer.

And that's because sharers give away all of the good stuff. And they do that because they want the world to be a better place. They want to share their gifts with the world so that others shine and others get notoriety and accolades.

So while being a sharer might not seem glamorous, the question I ask you is, of the two, who would you rather work for? Who would you rather have as a friend? As a mentor?

The answer is obvious to me. And the best friends I have ever had, and the mentors that have had the biggest influence on my life, are the sharers. They share for two reasons.

The biggest is that they are just good people. I feel like all of my friends would give you the shirt off their back if you needed it, without hesitation or expectation of repayment.

The other reason is because I would do the same for them. We have a symbiotic relationship where everybody wins, and everyone shares the spotlight.

So surround yourself with sharers. Work for them. Be friends with them. Because you deserve it.

Chapter 10
Use the Smell Test

We finally got the futon together. We stayed that night on Emily's couch. Mercifully, the electric company called us the following day to say the power was on. We moved in.

But KTXS still hadn't contacted me.

After we got everything settled in the apartment, I told Brad that I was going to go drop off my résumé at the other TV stations in town. KTXS was the ABC affiliate, so I assumed that there was at least a CBS and NBC station as well. We had no internet yet, so I went to the phone book. I looked in the Yellow Pages, and discovered that the NBC and CBS affiliates had the same address and phone number. I figured it was a typo, so I called the station, and they confirmed that both stations were in the same building.

Now, I am no expert in FCC regulations by any means, but it at the very least seemed odd. It was also pretty disheartening. It meant I had an even smaller chance to land a job if both stations were in the same building with the same boss reading the same résumés.

Remember that suit I wore on the car ride for the KTXS interview eight days ago? I threw it on the floor as soon as I got the chance. It was still crumpled up in the corner of the room. Not even laundered. So I did what any red-blooded American bachelor did. I smelled it and put it on. I picked up my manilla folder briefcase and set out to find gainful employment.

I probably should have scheduled an appointment or looked on a website to see if they had an opening. But my love of the movie moment where someone walks into a company and demands a job and refuses to leave until it happens, took over. I was desperate, but they had to see my passion and give me a job on the spot, right?

This was my second time ever in a news station. I walked in the door and froze. I didn't know who to ask for. I had no idea who to give my résumé to. I walked into a building that looked fairly normal on the outside, but the inside felt like the scene of a movie.

There were television screens everywhere with actual people on them delivering the news. It was surreal to know that they were probably less than 100 feet from me behind the walls of the reception room.

Have you ever been to a foreign country where you have no idea how to speak the language? You frantically look for someone in a crowd who speaks your language or at least would be able to translate your botched pronunciations. That's what it was like. I was in a place I knew nothing about. Sure, I'd had experience at the NFL and TVG networks, but sports stations and news stations might as well be on separate planets. There were news-specific terms, norms, phrases that were muscle memory for the people working there. I had to make the decision to either fake like I knew what I was talking about, or come clean and beg for mercy.

The look on the receptionist's face helped me make my decision.

She was probably about 16 years old. There was no way she had graduated from high school yet. Not that I looked older or more distinguished in my stale, oversized suit. I'm sure she could smell my despair from her perch at the desk. It was like she was staring into my soul. I wouldn't have been surprised if she had said, "You look like you've been having futon trouble recently. Let's sit down and talk about it."

I steeled myself and approached the desk.

"Hi, my name is Rob Mooring, and I am looking for a job. I have my résumé here, but I don't really know who to give it to."

She replied kindly, "No problem! I will give it to the News Director."

I responded, "The News Director! Of course! That's what I meant. That would be great."

We said goodbye, and I walked outside.

I walked out of the air-conditioned building and into the balmy

West Texas heat. A wave of despair washed over me. I felt like a complete idiot. I openly admitted to the high-school-aged gatekeeper of a news station that I had *no* idea what I was talking about. How could she think that I was fit to work at a news station, or even watch a news program for that matter?

I crumpled into the car and called Brad.

"I'm coming home to pack," I said. "The receptionist probably just threw my résumé into the trash along with the hundreds of others that came before me. There's no point in staying in Abilene if I can't get a job in TV."

It was a dark moment.

Brad, being the solid guy that he is, agreed to help me pack.

There was a real sadness between us that afternoon. We didn't really say much, which was weird for us, because normally it was hard to shut either of us up. I think we both had romanticized our Abilene excursion, and at this point it looked like it was coming to an end.

The Buster Moon Philosophy of Life

Pursuing your dreams is hard. And anyone that tells you differently is flat out wrong. It's not all sunshine and rainbows, and I hope at the very least this book gets that point across.

My kids love the movie *Sing*. It's a movie set in a strange humanoid animal world, kind of like Zootopia, but a musical.

The protagonist is a koala named Buster Moon. When he was a kid, his father would take him to the town's local theater, and little Buster ate it up. He dreamed that he would run the theater one day. His father saved up all the money he earned from his car washing job to help Buster achieve his dream.

When the story starts, Buster is in deep financial trouble because the theater isn't doing well, but you would never know it. His positivity and optimism is infectious. He has a friend named Eddie who is a sheep, and a realist. He sees Buster's impending financial doom and asks Buster how he is going to get out of it.

Buster replies simply with, "You know the great thing about hitting rock bottom? There's only one way left to go, and that's up!"

I cry every time he says that in the movie. It just resonates with me.

I don't pretend to know what you are facing; all I know is what happened to me. I was feeling the worst I had ever felt that day. It was the first time in my life that I hit rock bottom.

I hadn't really wanted to go off to college to start with, but I did. And with that decision came those intimidating life expectations of being "successful" and using my education. From my perspective at the time, I'd checked the boxes. I finished college. I had internships during school to give me some experience. I sent résumés and pursued the jobs I wanted.

And yet, in spite of checking all the boxes, a job was not easy to get. And on top of that, I'd just had a stressful couple of weeks.

With hindsight, I can see that this was just a minor step in the journey of my life, but my emotions at the time were so real. Before the Abilene failure sequence, I had been just like Buster Moon. Positive in the face of difficulty. But I had never felt this low before. I questioned my entire outlook on life. What would I do if I never got a job at a TV station?

The Call

What do you do when everything goes pear-shaped? How do you handle being faced with disappointment upon disappointment?

I had a friend who called me when I was in college. It was during my first year, so he asked the question everyone asked.

He said, "What are you going to major in?"

I told him that I was doing radio, television, and film. He laughed and immediately said, "Dude, you should *not* do that."

This guy was and is one of my best friends. I have known him for a long time, and he was coming from a really good place. He said that he had some experience working in the industry, and that the people tended to be pretty miserable. He said it didn't fit my personality to be around people like that, so I should think about something else.

It wasn't bad advice at all, and he was just being a good friend, but for some reason I just said thanks and moved on with my major.

With hindsight, that was clearly the right decision. But as I was packing up my car to leave Abilene and go back home, it didn't feel that way.

I wish I had some sort of magic solution for when you run into this in pursuit of your dreams, but I don't. I just want you to know that these days will exist. You will feel frustrated. You will feel like your efforts have been for nothing. In the moment, it will feel awful. It might be hard to push through, but you have to. Because one of two things happens. You get what you want, or you don't, and you get something different, something potentially better than you could have imagined.

Just know that those days and weeks and months and years exist. Recognize them for what they are. See them as opportunities for growth, not hurdles to clear, and you never know what could happen.

Chapter 11
I Won the Minimum Wage Lottery

In the midst of my existential crisis, the phone rang.

I got an interview. Then I got the job. All on the same day that I'd wondered if my sportscasting career was over before it had even started. Life moves fast at a small-time TV station.

My job title was Production Assistant. I would work 15 hours a week for $5.15 an hour.

It was not glamorous work. I would get in around 1:00 PM. My main objective was to find a guest for the next day's newscast to come and talk about a wide variety of things.

Once, and only once, did someone reach out to me and ask to be on the show. She had developed this tape to put on your muscles to help them feel better. I thought she was absolutely nuts. And now I see people wearing this stuff everywhere, so clearly she knew something that I didn't.

One of my bosses was the Producer of the 5 PM newscast, and she was a saint. She also knew that I loved sports, and she just so happened to be married to the Sports Director at the NBC station. She knew that's what I really loved, so as soon as I got my job done (usually in half an hour), I would race over to the sports desks of the two anchors and talk about sports. It was the absolute best part of my day. Those guys became *heroes* to me.

When I got home after finding out about the job, you would have thought I was just named CEO of NBC or something. Brad and I were celebrating, big time. We were happy because that job offer and his grad program were the rewards for our fights with futons and electric companies. We had made it to the other side. We had leveled up. And I landed a job in my dream career.

I remember calling my mom with the big news. Here's how the conversation went:

"Hey, mom. I got the job. It's not a great job, but it's a job." For some reason I felt equal parts excited and embarrassed. Had my parents sacrificed all this time, energy, and money for a college education for *this*? Had I worked so hard in college to be a part-time underling who wouldn't earn enough to pay for both rent and food? What would my mom say?

Not skipping a beat, she fired back, "Do you have health insurance?"

"Uhhhh no, but if I get a full-time job, I'll qualify for benefits."

She responded quickly, "Then get to it. Work hard and be kind."

It Ain't Exactly Rocket Science

I remember kind of rolling my eyes at my mom's words, but I have never been given better advice in all my life. The underlying message is this: don't treat a minimum wage job minimally.

Was it the job I thought I deserved? If you had asked me when I was still in college, I would have said no. Unequivocally. But it's funny how a few months in the real world changed my whole perspective.

For me, it was easy to take that job because I was desperate. The hiring guy could have told me that I was going to make fifteen cents an hour, and I probably would have taken it. It was certainly better than being unemployed all together.

Sure, it was an entry level job that they would give to a person without a college degree, but the entry was the cool part! I got to work at a real-life news station. I would see all of the behind-the-scenes action, and who knows, maybe work my way up to something incredible!

For all that positivity, there were some drawbacks. The most obvious one was the economics of the situation. My monthly expenses included $125 in college debt and $250 in rent. My income was a little over $200 a month after taxes. It doesn't take a mathematician to see that it didn't pencil out. My money was gone before I could even consider a budget for food, utilities, and meager entertainment. Thankfully, I had some money saved from summer jobs to tide me over until I could supplement the income.

And don't get me wrong; there are changes that need to be made. We should be able to have a minimum wage that provides a livable way of life, so that people are more free to take risks and chase their dreams.

And anyone who tells you that you need to "pick yourself up by the bootstraps" is a complete fool. Because most of the time that mantra is being hurled towards people who haven't been given a system that allows them to have "boots" at all.

But because I was a single man chasing my dream, I had the privilege of taking that job while simultaneously looking for another job to supplement my income. Had I been a father with a family and kids, no way. But I was lucky that I just had one mouth to feed, so it was easier for me to take the chance.

I recognize that privilege is not afforded to everyone, so knowing the obstacles you will face economically in chasing your dreams is essential to setting yourself up for success. For me, I had to swallow my idiotic pride as a college graduate and submit an application to Walmart until I had a full-time job. Those are the things you have to consider doing when chasing the things you really want.

The Call

Hopefully you won't be in a similar tax bracket when you leave college, but you might have a similar decision to face. Should I go after what I want, even if the pay is terrible? Or should I go for a safer job so I don't have to worry as much?

I know I keep coming back to this, but I think it's really important. Following your dream may not always be the most logical, easy, or financially secure path available to you. And yet, in my experience, it is worth pursuing.

Beyond that, building a career requires putting in hard work. It is easy to assume that because you have a college degree in your chosen field, you have all that you need to succeed. But the degree isn't the end of your learning about your career field. It is the beginning.

Your entry-level job, no matter what the title, is your chance to begin building your career. I did it by showing up, every day, with excitement and enthusiasm. And I wasn't faking it. I *loved* my job even though I was simultaneously checking my bank account every day to make sure I had lunch money.

Have you ever met someone who wasn't rich, but was still one of the happiest and most generous people you have ever met? These lucky people have found their passion, their vocation, their true calling in life, so they approach each day with a renewed enthusiasm that no paycheck can provide.

Finding that spark for me was instrumental to my development as a human being. Was it hard when I couldn't buy a measly pizza because my bank account was empty? Of course.

I feel like I have gotten the vast majority of breaks in my time on Earth because I am dependable and try and treat others with kindness. Will I become a millionaire by doing that? Probably not.

But I am pretty confident that I will always have a job just because I show up and work hard. I've never been the smartest, toughest, most competitive person at any job I've had, but I've been able to pay the bills.

I'm not sure if it's a cultural thing, a systemic political thing, or something else, but I feel like a lot of us in this country don't ever feel like what we do is enough.

There's always more money to make, a nicer car to have, a bigger house to live in, and more prestige to obtain. I'm not suggesting living outdoors in a hut or anything, but I feel like there is a lot of happiness to gain by being somewhere in between living in one of those micro homes on HGTV and having a mortgage payment that is more than most people make in a month. But I've never been rich, or owned a fancy car, or lived in a fancy house, so what do I know?

I think one of my college buddies said it best: "I don't think money is the root of all evil, but is it the root of all happiness?"

Regardless, I was proud of myself for not treating that minimum wage job minimally. I didn't work hard because I thought it would lead to more success; I worked hard because I loved it, and I was proud of the work I was doing. And that effort led to some truly incredible things.

When you are faced with a choice between following your passion and taking a safer route for financial stability, think about what you have to give up to have the "safer" route. Until we have an economic system in place to make chasing your dreams easier, it's a decision you are going to have to make. I took the risk, and it paid off in a big way.

81

Chapter 12
When in Doubt, Lie for a Good Cause

One of my main duties at my fancy new Production Assistant job
was delivering crudely made certificates done in Microsoft Word to
local restaurants. My other boss was the News Director, but he also
did a segment where he got the health department records for
restaurants. These records detailed whether restaurants had slime in
their ice machines or meat that wasn't heated to the appropriate
temperature. These are important points to consider when choosing
a place to eat. I found the segment completely unbearable, but the
locals loved it. For the restaurants that had an excellent report of
cleanliness, he printed out certificates of achievement. My job was
to put them in frames and drive around to deliver them. That
college degree at work, let me tell you.

One day as I was sitting in my boss's office putting paper into
frames, he got a call from the weekend sports anchor. My boss put
it on speaker; the anchor had quit. Just like that. No two weeks'
notice, nothing in writing, just quit over the phone. It was a
Thursday, and he was supposed to be on television on Saturday
night.

When I look back on this moment, I see God's hand at work. I
literally could have been anywhere else when the phone call arrived,
but for some reason I was in my boss's office, doing a menial task
that I didn't love, when opportunity came calling. My boss was a
nice man, but wasn't a bulldog when it came to finding talented
people. I honestly, truly believe that it didn't matter to him who was
sitting in that office, he probably would have asked anybody the
question he asked me. I just happened to be in the right place at the
right time.

He hung up the phone and turned to me, "Hey Rob, you did sports
broadcasting in college, right?"

There were no hard feelings toward the former weekend sports
anchor. In the world of small market, local news, this kind of
situation isn't all that rare. The combination of low wages and
sudden job openings does not create a culture of deep loyalty

among employees. Nor should it. So when an opportunity comes along, you have to jump on it. Quickly.

I had a decision to make in a split second. Should I lie and say that I had plenty of experience as a sports or news anchor even though I didn't? If he decided to check my résumé, he'd immediately discover the truth. Or should I do the right thing and tell him no for the good of the industry and the ethics of good journalism?

I said, "Of course! I did a lot of it in college actually."

His exact words were, "Great, why don't you fill in until we find a replacement. You start Saturday night. Good luck."

Kids and adults, I am not condoning lying, but it was an opportunity that I couldn't pass up. I wish I had some profound guilt because of what I did, or had some moment of clarity where I ran into the office and confessed, but it never came. This was my chance, and I knew I had to be extra prepared and excellent because I had never done what I was being asked to do. I had two days to figure out how to be a sports broadcaster.

At the time, I thought it was an impossible task. Forty-eight hours to figure out how to do a job, not to mention one that was on live television for thousands of viewers. You could have told me that I had 48 years to prepare for that first newscast, and I would have thought it wasn't enough time. But what I learned from this "baptism by fire" was that it was ideal that I didn't have time to properly prepare. If I'd had more time to really think, I would have psyched myself out. Instead, I just hoped that I would survive and prayed that no one was watching. This was my dream job, after all.

Because of that saint of a producer who was married to the sports director, I had the training I needed. He and the other anchor wrapped their arms around me and showed me the ropes. I hope they read this because they should know that if they had done the easy thing and blown me off, I wouldn't be writing these words right now. I know it seemed like a stretch when I called them heroes earlier, but it was the truth.

After a few weekends, my boss declared that I'd be the official weekend sports anchor.

I would be a full-time employee and get health benefits.

Obviously I called my mom right away. She was pumped; I mean she was seriously jacked up about it. Not about the fact that her beloved son was going to be on television, but that I could go to the Kelsey-Seybold clinic and get a flu shot for a reasonable price.

She was so excited that I didn't even get a chance to mention my salary boost. I got a raise from $5.15 an hour, to $7.15 an hour. Plus, all the fame that a small town could possibly provide. My trips to the local Walmart would never be the same. I honestly couldn't believe that someone was allowing me to be on television. It was surreal.

Listen to the Jedi

The moment when the News Director asked me if I had experience as a sports anchor was a big one. I mean it was huge, and it was for reasons I didn't even know about at the time. But it could have easily gone the other way.

What if I had said no?

What if I had listened to "The Resistance"?

I stole "The Resistance" term from a friend of mine. Another one from the guy who talked me into writing this book. I was considering a career change, and he suggested that I get feedback from others about my strengths. Once I had it, we sat down at a hamburger joint to talk about my future. This friend is really good at knowing what I am thinking, right as I am thinking it. It's freaky, in a Jedi Mind Trick kind of way.

We sat down for about 45 minutes. We talked about my strengths, and then he laid it out for me. He said that I had a gift, and not using and developing it would be stealing from humanity. I didn't say anything, but I was thinking that seemed incredibly dramatic. I just listened politely, knowing what was actually going to happen after the meeting.

Then he used his powers to peer into my mind, and he called me on it.

He told me that as soon as I walked out of the restaurant, maybe even before I made it to the door, I would convince myself that writing a book was impossible.

Somehow he knew that I had already convinced myself it was impossible. We hadn't even finished our conversation yet!

That, my friends, is "The Resistance." It is the voice in your head that tells you any number of disheartening things in order to convince you not to follow your dreams.

The Call

We humans are prone to listening to "The Resistance." We're wired that way. On a basic level, it is a legit survival mechanism. The problem arises when we let the negative talk constantly run the show and use it as an excuse to take the easy route.

When it came to the sports anchor job, I had almost no time to think about it. I didn't even give "The Resistance" a chance to talk me out of taking a chance. But in other instances throughout my life, like with writing this book, "The Resistance" has taken over hard core.

Here's what that sounds like:

I'd love to write a book. Sure. But what if I write a book, and people think it is horrible, which they probably will? And worse yet, what if the book exposes the fact that I am a fraud and know nothing about life or anything? I've certainly failed publicly before (see college orientation stunt), but not in such a vulnerable way. I'm not sure this is a risk I'm willing to take.

Sound familiar at all?

Sometimes the best thing we can do is get out of our own way. It's easier said than done. For me, it took relative strangers I really respected to tell me that I could write a book. Strangers is not a typo.

I am lucky to have family, friends, and a wife who encourage me and believe in me. They always tell me that I am destined for great things, or that I should have invented something awesome by now. I appreciate their support, but to some degree, I feel like they have to say that. They are somehow legally and morally bound to be nice to me. So I don't trust their feedback as much. It's not a "them" problem, it's a "me" problem.

The catch-22 of all of this is that in order for strangers to give me feedback, good or bad, I have to give strangers something to judge. I have to be vulnerable in front of people I don't know very well. That is a very scary thing. But if the feedback from strangers fuels my professional soul, I would be an idiot not to give this book thing a try right?

Remember Chancellor Runnels? The guy who started YCS and thus changed the course of my life forever? He passed away recently. I remember where I was when I got the call. I was devastated.

The family reached out to me and asked that I speak on behalf of YCS at Chancellor Runnels' memorial service.

I thought for sure that they had dialed the wrong number.

I agreed to be polite, but I was absolutely terrified. There would be *lots* of people in attendance, and what credibility did I have to summarize this incredible man's legacy?

As I sat in the front row at the memorial, I looked at the program. I noticed that Pepperdine's volleyball coach was speaking, and if you know anyone that plays volleyball, just say the name Marv Dunphy, and you'll have instant credibility. He is a volleyball legend. He spoke before me.

There was also an opera singer who sang before me. He crushed it.

You could tell that the person that introduced me felt really sorry for me. The scheduling gods had set me up for complete failure.

I got up, said some words I don't remember, and sat down. I breathed a sigh of relief and figured that would be the end of it.

It was, until this lady grabbed me by the arm as I was walking out.

She was a stranger, so she apologized for grabbing me. Then she said something that changed how I felt about myself forever.

She said, "I want you to know that your speech was incredible. You were the best person up there. Bar none."

My wife, my mom, my siblings, my best friends could have all said the same thing, and I wouldn't have believed it. But this stranger gave me a boost to my self-confidence that I hadn't felt before.

I realized that the best feedback you can get from someone could be from a stranger. Because they know you the least, and they have the least knowledge about what will happen next. They aren't invested in your life emotionally, so their opinion comes with the least baggage, and it just might be the most genuine.

It's not easy or fun to be vulnerable, but it's the key to growth. I have to be willing to put myself out there. And if the whole endeavor turns out to be a failure, well, it won't be the end of the world.

But what if it works? The lady in the audience thought it did, and that further catapulted me into the idea of writing this book.

Think about how you will respond when opportunity knocks. How will you know when to say yes and when to say no? You've probably failed dozens of times and lived through it, but you just never thought about it beyond when it happened because it hurt. But that pain from vulnerability can lead to incredible things. So take a chance, because why can't it be you?

Someone out there is doing what you were meant to do because they believed they could. So why can't you do the exact same thing?

Chapter 13
Get a Less Distracting Camera Person

A few weeks later, the weeknight sports anchor, who I thought was the coolest man on the planet (still do), said that he and his wife were going out of town, and asked if I could fill in for his sportscast on a Tuesday. You talk about excited. I was going to be on air with the big boys and girls. No more sitting at the kids' table on the weekend sportscast. No more having to cover a bike rodeo because a news anchor called in sick. I had hit the big time.

I sat in the chair, did my mic check, and then proceeded to make a complete hash of it.

It was one of the worst newscasts I had ever done. But it wasn't my fault. There was a new girl behind the camera, and she was completely distracting me. I finished doing the show, and as soon as she walked out, I turned to the meteorologist and said, "Who was that girl?"

He explained to me that he had met her at the Taylor County Fair, because of course you do a live broadcast from a county fair in Texas. She came up to him and said that it had always been her dream to be a newscaster, and that she would do anything for a chance. He talked to her for a little while and gave her the number for the production manager so that she could maybe start on a camera or in the booth, to get exposure to the business. She jumped at the opportunity and got the job quickly. He told me her name was Stephanie.

There Used to Be These Things Called Video Stores

What I didn't think about when becoming the weekend sports anchor was that I would work on the weekends. Every weekend. My days off were Tuesday and Wednesday. Do you know who else on planet Earth has Tuesdays and Wednesdays off? Other weekend newscasters. That's it. So my social life wasn't all that exciting.

One lonely Tuesday, I got the bright idea to drive around town and find something to do. There was a local video store close to our apartment called Box Office Video. I decided to go in and start an account so I could pass the time watching movies. Every real adult at that time had a movie rental account. It seemed like a rite of passage I was ready to experience.

The lady behind the counter was really nice. I think I rented the first season of "Lost". Being the responsible adult that I was, I returned it several days late. When I came back, there was a man behind the counter who was about 6'4", and one of the friendliest people I had ever met. He struck up a conversation almost instantly as I came through the door. Eventually I told him that I worked at KRBC as a sports anchor. I couldn't believe the next thing he said:

"You work at KRBC? Get out of town! My daughter just got a job there."

A sudden overwhelming fear and anxiety took over my body. Surely, of all the video stores in all the world, this was not Stephanie the smoke show camera operator's father.

"Oh that's cool! What's her name?" I asked, already suspecting the answer.

"Her name is Stephanie, and she is running a camera I think. Do you know her?"

"Um, yeah, I think I have seen her around. Tell her I said hello."

Smooth.

I also found out in that conversation that the nice lady that helped me set up my account the week before was Stephanie's mom, Paula, and her father, the man I was trying to play it cool with, was John.

I took it as a sign. I had talked to Stephanie a few times at the station, but never for more than a few minutes. When I saw her next time at the TV station, I tried to lay down my best game. Here's how it went:

"Hey Stephanie, how are you?"

She replied, "I'm doing all right, how are you?"

"I'm great!" I said, cringing at my own over-enthusiasm. I regained my composure, and continued, "I mean yeah, I am doing ok. Hey, I think I met your parents...and if I am honest, I kind of like them more than I like you."

"Oh. Okay," she replied in horror.

I was instantly filled with shame and regret. Who in their right mind would say such a thing and expect another human being to think it was funny or even remotely conversational? I would have been better off saying almost anything else. Hell, I could have said that I have 14 hamsters, and she would have found that more attractive than me telling her she stinks and her parents are awesome. Why didn't I just say "hi" and leave it at that? So much for playing it cool.

I went home dejected, nursing a self-inflicted wound.

Still My Toy Guitar Gently Weeps

A couple of weeks passed, and on another Tuesday I was at home playing Guitar Hero, because every cool kid was doing it. I hadn't showered in a while, I was in my pajamas, it was 3:30 in the afternoon, and I had a pizza sauce stain from the Totino's I just ate. I was really firing on all cylinders.

As soon as I finished my song, I had a moment of clarity. I thought to myself, "Who are you? Why are you sitting here, by yourself, covered in filth, and playing a game designed for 8-year-olds, when you could go talk to a real, live human being?"

I took a shower, threw on my best t-shirt, and drove to the station. I hoped to catch Stephanie as she walked in, because you know, that's how it worked in "You've Got Mail". Plus, if I met her outside I wouldn't be humiliated in front of our coworkers when she told me to get lost.

I stood around awkwardly outside until another station employee walked by and asked what I was doing there on my day off. I said I was hoping to catch Stephanie. The coworker informed me that Steph was in the control room. I considered jumping back in my car and heading home, but I'd already made the drive. And showered. And changed my shirt.

I made my way to the control room and found her with eight other production crew members. I had to go into the belly of the beast. With witnesses.

I don't know if it was because I was feeling courageous or a little too overconfident after my shredding sesh on Guitar Hero, but I walked into the control room, asked her for her number, and she gave it to me. I thought it was surely a fake, because she was WAY too pretty to give me the real one, but she did. And we went out on our first date.

It didn't go well. For some reason, I decided it would be a good idea to take her to get a snow cone in February. It was really cold. I wouldn't say the date was terribly awkward or anything, but it certainly wasn't a fireworks show.

Afterward, we didn't talk for six months. And we worked at the same place. Talk about awkward.

The Call

No matter how much you think you've figured out about your life, there's always something else to learn. In the above situation, it was how to successfully converse with potential romantic partners. But that wasn't the first "real world" thing I had to learn, and it wasn't the last.

Having worked in college counseling for several years, I've come up with some tips on this topic. The broad theme is that I think it's important to not specialize your life. Or at least not to specialize your life too early.

There's a popular figure of speech that I find revolting:

"Jack of all trades, master of none."

The most ironic part of that idiom is that the "master of none" part was not part of the original saying. It was added later in America, which makes perfect sense. I'll get into that in a minute.

The saying was actually jack of all trades in and of itself at first, and it started as a compliment. It was famously used in a derisive way in the late 1500's by an English author named Robert Greene. He wrote an entry in a booklet making fun of a guy, and used the term. Guess who he was talking about?

William Shakespeare.

Billy. Effing. Shakespeare. Robert Greene, whose name I didn't know until today, made fun of William Shakeaspeare for being a jack of all trades. Can you imagine something more foolish?

The idea of specializing your career and your life is an epidemic I wish I had the cure for. It leads people to follow careers for money and comfort, and not for passion and relationships. It takes the fun out of it, and when you work for a living, fun can be a hard thing to come by. This idea of specialization leads politicians to say things like "We need more welders and fewer philosophers."

The most awful thing about saying that is you discount both of those trades with that view. You obviously discount the importance of people that study philosophy, but in a weird way, you make an assumption that welders aren't capable of deep, critical thought. I bet 99% of welders are smarter and more talented than I am. Same for philosophers.

But here is the key difference for me. I have had a lot of kids tell me that they wanted to become welders because welders "make good money." Which I think can be true. But the bigger question is, what does "good money" mean? How much is it? What is the difference between a livable wage and a "good" one?

The other thing that worries me about kids specializing in something and immediately entering a trade is what if, after 10 years, they are tired of welding? Then what? They have to essentially start from scratch. My degree, right or wrong, has given me a wide variety of options to choose from, and I have been in different career paths due to that piece of paper and the previous experience I've had.

A lot of people say, "Well, college isn't for everyone." But if you ask those same people if they want their kids to go to college, they almost always say yes. And because of the hypocrisy of those people, I worry that other kids and their families-families that don't have the same history of attending college-will stay away because they think it's not worth the investment, or they are worried about how marketable their college degree will be.

And I get both of those things, but all I can say to counter that thinking are the three reasons I want my kids to go to college.

The first reason is that I want them to be around people who don't look like them, think like them, act like them, or talk like them. I want them to be challenged and pushed beyond their comfort zone whether it's in politics, race, or anything else for that matter. Surrounding yourself with people that are *just* like you is the best way to impede personal growth.

The second reason is because grade school sucks. It just isn't that fun. I want to help my kids go to college as a reward for getting through kindergarten and senior year alike. I want them to be out on their own, to enjoy themselves as much as possible before they enter the workforce, which ironically, is kind of like grade school. You show up to the same place every day, do the same thing, and repeat.

But the most important reason that I want my kids to go to college is because I want them to learn about random things they wouldn't have otherwise. I want them to study things because they choose to, and I want them to learn from an eclectic group of professors and students. I want to send them to college so that they *aren't* specialized, so that they aren't one-trick ponies, and so that they can realize that the path from being born to achieving success isn't a straight line, nor should it be.

To me, a liberal arts education offers flexibility and comfort. It allows students to learn about a lot of different things, and hopefully along the way find a passion that makes them happy. I took classes in things that I wouldn't have ever chosen to, but was forced to because of the curriculum. And thank God I was. Even if the subject matter didn't resonate with me, I met fellow students and professors who were impactful in my growth as a human being. I think the liberal arts model allowed me to be a better version of myself and a better conversationalist. I learned a little about a lot of things, so I am typically perceived as interesting in conversations and job interviews. I owe the vast majority of that to my education at Pepperdine. But you don't have to go to college in order to reap those benefits; you just have to be curious and willing to learn about new things to better yourself.

So keep learning. Don't specialize. Be diverse in your thinking and in your compassion, and you never know what might come your way. College isn't the end of your education. It's the place you go to get good at learning and interacting with people who are different than you.

Chapter 14
Warm Water, Strong Legs, Can't Lose

Obviously, after my romantic setback, I reaffirmed my devotion to the task of building my sportscasting career. After that interview with Al Michaels, I had a singular, some might say specialized, path. Nothing was going to stop me.

The only problem was, by this point, I *was* a sports anchor, so what was I supposed to do now? Was this what I worked so hard for? If so, I had to admit there was something underwhelming about it.

I remembered a speech I'd heard from a guy named Jimmy Weldon at YCS. He was always one of my favorites. One of the things he always told us was never to become a bullfrog.

He described a scientific experiment involving frogs. You've probably heard of it before. In this experiment, scientists placed a beaker full of water over a Bunsen burner and heated it to boiling. Next they dropped a frog into the water to see how it would react. As you might expect, a frog dropped into hot water jumps out.

In the second part of the experiment, scientists filled up the same beaker with room temperature water and put the frog in it. Since the water was comfortable, the little frog subjects relaxed in the beaker. The poor frogs didn't even notice the heat gradually increasing. They boiled alive.

Fun fact: this story is not actually true. Real scientists pretty much agree that frogs can sense rising temperatures and will move if they are uncomfortably warm. And if you threw them in boiling water they'd likely be too badly injured to get out.

But real science aside, the point remains relevant.

Don't be complacent. You can get comfortable in your surroundings. It creeps up on you before you even realize it. I had only been a sports anchor for a few months, but I was already starting to feel like the bullfrog.

I was getting good at my job, so much so that it was becoming easy and formulaic. I loved the people I worked with, and I was figuring out how to live on not a lot of money. And all of that was comfortable, so I hardly looked outside of my surroundings to grow and evolve. I had made it. My dream was realized.

But it didn't feel like enough.

After some reflection, I finally concluded that it didn't feel like enough because I wasn't sharing the best version of myself with someone else. It was just me, and I was already used to just me. Before Steph came along, I didn't even think about how someone else could change my plan. I wouldn't have even considered allowing it to happen. I honestly didn't even consider marriage and family to be in the cards for me at all.

Sure, dating seemed fun, but not real commitment. It's not hard to imagine that I had a fear of commitment. My parents' marriage was volatile and violent, so I never held out much hope for a real relationship of my own.

Instead of worrying about starting a family, I focused on my career. I put blinders on all things other than that, because to be honest, I didn't want to get hurt. And if the pursuit of my job hurt me, that was my own doing. I was in control.

Résumé Version #119

I have a brother-in-law named Tyler that I have known since I was 9 years old. He was my sister's high school sweetheart, and they have been married ever since. When I was young, he worked at this miniature golf place in Houston called Putt-Putt. He was the go-cart manager, which I thought was the coolest job on the planet. Whenever I was there, he would bring me a Pepsi cup full of tokens, and I would spend hours in the arcade. And when you're 9, and someone gives you an endless supply of tokens, that person is a legend.

As devastating as it was when he quit his job at Putt-Putt to start his career, he's someone I have always looked up to and tried to model myself after. And of all the positive qualities to admire about him, there is one that stands out above the rest.

I don't know how many versions of his résumé he has, but it has to be a considerable number.

That's because Tyler changes jobs. A lot. Whenever he gets tired of what he is doing, or wants a chance to make a better living to support his family, he puts himself out there. He updates his résumé, looks around, and finds a different job.

There are two main reasons why that idea has been successful for Tyler. The first is that he is not risk-averse. He is willing to try something new, or work with different people, to get the outcome he wants. He also is willing to accept rejection if it comes down to that, and he doesn't let rejection defeat or define him.

And the other reason is that he is super self-aware. He knows what his talents are, and he knows how to articulate his strengths and weaknesses in interviews. He is vulnerable enough to talk about what value he brings to his company and the things he is still trying to learn.

Before I went for my first big job interview, I asked Tyler for advice, and he gave me one of the best tips I have ever heard. He said two things, to ask questions about the company, which required doing homework to learn about the company's values and priorities, and he said to ask one question at the end. He told me to ask, "Is there any reason why you are hesitant to hire me?"

Talk about courage! People have always told me not to ask questions I don't want to know the answer to. Is the question risky? Sure. It has the potential to hurt your pride or feelings.

But on the flip side, the question is fantastic for a couple of reasons. One, it gives you the chance to rebuke any doubts they have about you. And they probably aren't going to flat out tell you what they think your limitations are, but when you ask them, they are more likely to respond to your question.

But the second reason has come to fruition for me more times than not. I think it's given the hiring manager the confirmation that I am right for the job because they might think to themselves, "Well, I can't think of a reason *not* to hire this person."

Whether or not that seals the job for you, who knows, but at least it gets them thinking about giving it to you. It's like subliminal messaging at the movies. It might not get you to buy popcorn, but it will probably get you to the snack bar.

The Call

I had a student come into my office during August of senior year, right before she was about to get started on college applications. She had a panicked look on her face. It seemed like she was about to hyperventilate when she stopped, gathered her breath, and forced out, "Mr. Mooring, I don't think I am going to get into college at all."

I assured her that things were going to be fine, and that we would apply to a nice balance of schools so that she had options to choose from. But she was insistent that she was going to get denied *everywhere*.

For her, the fear of hearing "no" was far more powerful than the hope of hearing "yes". She was terrified of the no, as if getting denied to a school would be an indictment of her intelligence and potential. Spoiler alert: it isn't.

With my guidance and reassurance, she applied to seven of the ten schools on her list, all of which would let her know around Christmas time.

As the months passed, I didn't hear a lot from her, but as we started getting into December, I would see her every few days. And every few days, she would come by and tell me that she had gotten into a college. And after the dust settled before Christmas break, she had gotten into every single school. All seven of them.

I was so thrilled for her and was so excited to see her when she got back from Christmas break. All her fears had been relieved, or so I thought.

I saw her the first day back at school, and she looked nervous-and sad. I asked her what was wrong, and she said, "I know I have three more schools to hear from, but now I am kind of hoping I *don't* get in, because if I do, then that just makes the decision harder."

I was flabbergasted. I couldn't believe what I was hearing. She wanted to get denied?

But as I thought more about it, it made total sense to me. She had probably already made a decision in her mind, she had controlled the narrative to this point, but if one or all of the other schools admitted her, then what? And what if she made a *bad* decision? Would she live the rest of her life with regret in her choice?

Looking back on my time in Abilene, when I had "made it", I was the exact same way. I was in control. But it was a complete illusion.

I had become a bullfrog. I had gotten so comfortable with my life that the thought of anything interrupting it was out of the question. So I was hesitant with my feelings towards Stephanie because she was a "threat" to my comfort; she was making me feel out of control of my career and my life.

And what if I fell in love with her? And what if we got married? And then 10 years later, we got divorced? What if I made a *bad* decision?

I believe that we are far more likely to *create* a bad decision, than *make* a bad decision.

I see this all the time with my students. They get their college list down to two or three schools, and they are so worried about the decision that they struggle to make one at all. They think there is some soulmate college out there that will be perfect for them, and if they don't pick that school, then their college experience will suffer. And how are they supposed to know which school is their soulmate?

I got news for you. I lived in Malibu for college. Our campus looked like a dad-gum timeshare, and there were days when I swore to myself that I had made the wrong decision.

There are days like that in marriage, too. In my job, too.

But the difference between making a bad decision and creating one comes down to attitude and action.

I tell my students that when you have your first crappy day, or week, or even month in college, you create a bad decision by feeling sorry for yourself and doing nothing to change it.

I think it's the same with marriage, too. If at the first sign of trouble, you think of ways to jump ship instead of dive in, then you are headed down a road to disaster.

Holding onto the comfort and predictability of my life might have helped me in the short term, but it was impeding my growth. Not just in my career, but in my personal life. When I learned to let go of that control, and take a risk in both my work and my personal life, my world became truly meaningful and whole.

Chapter 15
Play Faire, or Don't Play at All

One day, as I was walking into the men's restroom at work, Steph was walking out of the women's restroom. She stopped me and said, "Hey Rob, we should hang out again sometime. You still have my number, right?"

Of course I had her number. I had practically made xerox copies of it and put it into a safety deposit box.

The funny thing was, I was kind of dating someone else when I had this interaction. She lived in a different city, so we saw each other every few weeks or so.

But as soon as Steph and I had this interaction at the bathroom, I immediately ran around the corner, called the girl I was seeing, and told her we were done.

Just like that. Not my finest hour.

So I called Steph a few days later, and we went on another date.

This one went better. We played mini golf at a place called Play Faire Park, famed for being the oldest miniature golf course in Texas. It instantly became our favorite place.

When we went to Play Faire, it felt like we were in a completely different city or state. It was quirky and strange, and a place where everyone felt welcome, all the time.

The guy who runs it, a man named Dan, became one of our favorite people. Here is a picture of me, Steph, and Dan during one of our dates.

In the photo, Steph is pleading with me to go to a haunted house with her that was attached to Play Faire, and I am refusing because I hate things that scare me. Which is a fair argument.

Steph and Dan's counterargument was...it was run by a local church. A church youth group had designed the entire thing, so I can't imagine it was scary at all. That argument was also fair.

The more we visited and the more we got to know Dan, it became obvious that he was running Play Faire Park because he *loved* to run it. He loved to be there. He loved having a place where families came to hang out, to get away from their screens, and be together.

Dan would book local bands to play at night. He had Saturday tie-dye shirt making events. Dan had lived in Abilene his whole life, and it was clear that he loved the community.

So he didn't do it for the money. He did it for the joy of building relationships. He wasn't a rich man, but his joy and love of life was infectious.

So if Dan can dedicate his life to something like that, then why couldn't I dedicate myself to that wonderful woman in the picture that was pleading with me to enter a not-so-haunted house?

I felt like I had won the lottery with this woman. And apparently other people agreed.

Case in point, I was going to interview a high school football coach

one time, and Steph had the day off, so she came with me. I knew
the coach well because I interviewed him every week. As I walked
up with Stephanie, he said hello, and I introduced them to each
other.

He shook her hand, and gave me a puzzled glance. In a thick, West-
Texas drawl, he said, "Boy…you out-punted yer coverage didn't
ya?"

I sure did.

Steph and I connected over our love of working in news. And make
no mistake, she is a better person than I am in every conceivable
way. When she was a kid, she worked at her parents' video stores.
She always had a dream of becoming a news anchor. So when
nobody was in the store, she would pick up one of the DVD cases
and turn it to the back. Each movie would have a summary of the
film, and she would read it like it was a real news story. Unlike me,
Stephanie knew what she wanted from a young age and stopped at
nothing to get it.

Part of Stephanie's job every day was to pick up a copy of the
scripts for the director. The printer was right behind the desk of the
news anchor, an absolute Abilene legend. He worked at the news
station before it was on television. He is an institution, and a
wonderful man.

Stephanie took the opportunity of being near him to talk to him
about his life and his career. He was impressed with her dream and
wanted to help her. After the news concluded, Stephanie would
stick around and practice reading stories from the news desk, and
the anchor would give her feedback. I admired her for her
determination. In spite of my reservations about relationships in
general, there was a magnetic pull between Steph and me that I
couldn't ignore.

In every other relationship I had ever had, I never felt safe. My
parent's dysfunctional relationship was the only example I had to
glean from, so my fear of commitment was founded on actual
evidence. Not based on a huge sample size, but it was all I had to go

on.

But being around Stephanie was different. She was brilliant, strong, courageous, opinionated, and all of those things made her great. But what made her special was her love of kids. She couldn't wait to be a mom, and she would take care of her nephew constantly. She felt at peace with a baby in her arms, and it was something that I hadn't experienced before in a relationship. I felt so at ease with her, and at the same time, admired her immensely. She *went* for things, took risks, and did it without fear.

Love and the Magic Bullet

I will never forget the first time we went to her parents' house. Stephanie was born in Abilene and grew up and went to school in a town called Merkel. Merkel's current population is 2,600.

We were dating, and it was around Thanksgiving time. My family wasn't big on the holiday, but Steph's family was, so she invited me over. We drove through Merkel, and it was like traveling back in time.

The streets downtown are made of cobblestone. There are exactly zero stop lights in Merkel. Only a flashing yellow that's adjacent to what they describe as a grocery store. Merkel had this charm that is hard to describe and hard to imagine unless you experience it. Life is slower there, and there are some real benefits to that.

Steph and her family lived in a home on a plot of land. Her uncle and aunt lived on the next plot at the time, and her grandmother lived on the next plot over. It was the first time I had really seen a cow up close because Steph's parents owned some. Many of them were named after grandkids or family members.

Their home was so friendly and welcoming. When we walked in, everyone was huddled around the TV screen playing a live action version of the game *Scene It*, which is a movie trivia game. Steph quickly introduced me to everyone, but nobody really stopped playing the game. They were so into it, and I *loved* that.

There was a question type that looked like the Wheel of Fortune board. There was a category at the top and blank spaces where letters should go. Eventually they would reveal one letter at a time until someone guessed the right answer.

I felt overmatched because these were *movie* people. I mean they owned movie rental stores for crying out loud. And the category was Classic Cinema. I knew I was out of place in so many ways, so I decided I'd leave this round to the professionals. Then this question came up. It looked like this:

Classic Cinema

___ ___ ___ ___   ___ ___ ___ ___   ___ ___ ___ ___

I had a complete out of body experience. Before any letters came up, I shouted, "Cool Hand Luke!"

There was silence, and everyone turned and looked at me.

Have you ever had that dream where you go to school, and you get up to do your speech, and you realize you forgot to wear pants? Remember that feeling of utter shame and embarrassment?

That's what this was like. I had no idea what the reaction would be. What happened next told me everything I needed to know.

All of them, in a West Texas slang, yelled versions of "Who is this guy? Who brought this fancy city slicker to this house to rig this game???"

It was a riot. I knew I had found another family I could belong to. It made me fall deeper in love with Stephanie.

My sisters had been married for years when all of this was happening to me, and before I met Steph, I always asked them about how they knew they were in love with their husbands.

They gave me the absolute dumbest answer. They told me, "When you know, you just know."

That answer seemed like complete balderdash at the time. But then Steph and I hung out one night.

She was still living with her brother, and they didn't have cable, so our options were limited. It was probably around 11 at night, so we were watching an infomercial for "The Magic Bullet", which is a high-powered blender.

As we were watching, she reached over and grabbed my hand. And then in an instant, my life changed forever.

She squeezed my hand tightly. Almost as if to say, "I love you, and I am glad you are here."

That was it. My sisters were right. I fell in love with Steph right then and there. And I should have realized it was true because I knew moving to Abilene was the right thing to do. I had fallen in love with the idea of moving to West Texas, just like I was falling in love with my girlfriend. There wasn't a sign, or some sort of buzzer that sounded when I was in love. I just knew. My sisters were right.

If you had told me that another person would change the way I thought about my dream, then I would have called you crazy. And that had everything to do with my childhood.

"Erase your name off of your birth certificate. I don't want you as a son anymore."

Those were the last words my father said to me. That was 18 years ago.

For most of my youth, my dad yelled. He yelled at my mom, my sisters, sometimes me. He had demons that were fueled by alcohol and drug addiction. He was manipulative, cruel, and an abuser. He is a terrible person whom I hold no sympathy for, and that's hard because I like to think that I am a pretty understanding guy. What he did was beyond understanding, though. The fact that my sisters turned out to be wonderful mothers and human beings is a demonstration of immeasurable human strength.

The thing about love is, it doesn't give a damn about what's in your control or what your history might be. Meeting Stephanie and falling in love with her made me forget about all the bad things that could happen to us if we went down the road of marriage. I knew my feelings were real because I didn't hesitate to see myself with her for the rest of my life. It felt natural. It just felt right.

Steph and I dated for two months before I knew I was madly in love with her. Even though I was ready, she still needed some time. About a month. We dated three months and then I proposed. She said yes. We've been married ever since. It was 13 years ago this past summer.

The Call

One of my colleagues graduated from law school and now works at our high school. I was always fascinated by that because reinventing yourself is something that I think is really cool.

So I finally sat down and asked her about the path to where she is now. She said that when she was a freshman in college, she had a document on her computer called "The Plan." It was a complete and meticulous breakdown of every semester, and then every year after, of her life.

And in all of the words on that document, none of them contained discussion around working as an administrator at a high school.

She told me that the grand plan that she made got blown up when her mom got sick and everything changed.

Do you know what is ironically missing in most people's life plan?

Life.

And life is not completely under our control, no matter how much we would like it to be.

We get so hyper-focused on the A and Z of our lives that we forget about letters B-Y. That's the problem with trying to plan out your whole life when you're 18 years old. You can't possibly predict everything that will happen to you. You can't predict how you will change. You can't predict the people you will meet. The twists and turns in my opinion make life most exciting and interesting. Those twists and turns bring us to opportunities and people we never would have found otherwise. That is, if we allow ourselves to even consider the possibility of our plan being--gasp--wrong.

Another one of the wisest things my mom said to me as a kid was, "Rob, if you want to make the good Lord laugh, tell Him your plans."

I always rolled my eyes at her because what preceded these words of wisdom was me trying to get out of going to church or out of something I didn't want to do, but should have done. She was absolutely right.

And it doesn't have to be God. It can be anything that guides you.

I am not saying that you should jump from place to place or job to job with no rhyme or reason, but I also think that closing yourself off to other places and other people because you've crossed off everything on your life to-do list is a dangerous thing. And if you do it, you might be a bullfrog.

What I am saying is don't be afraid to change your plan when something incredible happens to you. It's easy to get hyper-focused on work or ourselves and be totally blind to something or someone practically hammering you over the head, trying to get your attention and lead you to a life you never knew you could have. Don't be afraid to adapt or change for yourself. In fact, plan to change in ways that you can't even predict.

Chapter 16
Have Sleeping Bag. Will Squat.

Steph and I honeymooned in California. Of course, I took her to
Pepperdine so that I could show her how cool I was in college.
After not buying that for a single second and touring campus, she
had this peculiar look on her face. I couldn't quite read it. I asked,
"So what do you think?"

She turned to me with the most serious face she had given me at
that point in our marriage and said, "If you don't move me here in
the next three years, I'm coming without you."

Compelling.

When we got back to Abilene, things were great. We were living the
dream. We were both local news anchors in a small town. Talk
about a power couple.

Our trips to Walmart were different experiences for each of us,
though.

Steph got stopped everywhere she went. You would have thought
the governor of Texas was in the store that day. People just wanted
to meet her, shake her hand, and tell her how much they loved
having her in their home.

That was always what people said, and it struck me as odd. They
acted like because they turned their TV on, they were inviting you
into their home. Like we knocked on your door with a sleeping bag
in hand, ready to exercise our squatting rights or something.

And never, not once, did someone talk to Steph about how much
they loved her, and then turn to me and say how much they loved
me on the news. Never. Their question always was, "Now who is
this with you?"

WE WERE ON THE SAME NEWSCAST.

I should not have been surprised. Steph has always outshined me and always will. It's better this way. The future is female anyhow.

The Show

A crazy thing happened early in our marriage. The main sports guy, who again I thought was the coolest dude on the planet, moved to a different city with his wife, who also worked at the station. So the boss called me into his office and announced that I was the Interim Sports Director.

I was now the main guy! No more having Tuesdays and Wednesdays off with the rest of the motley crew of weekend news personalities. No more spending Saturdays dripping in sweat on a football field. And more time to eat bougie brunches at the Cracker Barrel on Sunday mornings. I had made it.

And so had Steph. We were Abilene's news couple. One time Steph forgot to put on her wedding ring for the newscast. She got several emails asking about our relationship, and if it was okay. At least that's what she told me they said. My guess is that they threatened to hurt me if I had ever wronged her, but I think she censored it for me.

Now that we were flying high in our careers, we were ready to plant our roots. We bought a house pretty close to the station. It was a total fixer upper, and we loved every minute of that home remodel.

It fit our budget too. At our prime, I was making $7.50 hourly, and Steph had just renegotiated her contract. The rival station (the one with the judgy lady in the slinky shirt) had called her out of the blue, because they knew their main news anchor was leaving. They offered her a job. They said they would pay her $26,000.

You would have thought we had won the lottery. We could not *imagine* what we would do with all that money. We were already shopping for retirement communities in Boca Raton.

But Steph was undeterred. She said to me, "I am going to use this as leverage. I am going to tell our boss that I got offered this job, and if they don't pay me $28,000, I'll walk."

I almost fainted. I looked at her like, *are you a crazy person?* There was no way they would give her that much. I told her she might as well start packing her desk. They would be so insulted by such a figure.

But being the strong woman she is, she went in confidently, and they gave her the money.

At that point, we just started lighting dollar bills on fire. We had made it to the high life and then some. Being young and naive is a beautiful thing.

With that windfall of cash, we bought our first home together on Poplar Street. We affectionately called it "The Debbie House" because the lady that lived there before was named that. The first time we looked at the house, we knocked on Debbie's door, and she let us right in. We looked around, and I noticed that her closet had a lock on it. It was on the outside of the door.

I said, "Hey Miss Debbie, why is there a lock on this door?"

She replied immediately, "Well for the ghosts, of course."

We moved in. We were so broke that we put a 30-year mortgage on a house we bought for $41,000. That house had character, and so did the neighborhood.

Our next-door neighbor made our acquaintance one day by knocking on the front door. She introduced herself as Bubbles. I kid you not.

Bubbles asked if she could use our bathroom. We found the request odd, but we said of course. She came in, used the restroom, and left a used cigarette butt in the bathtub.

She came by many times after that.

Doesn't all that sound idyllic? We had great jobs, a happy marriage, and a house with ghosts and interesting neighbors. Life was good.

A Star Is Born?

Remember how I said I was the *Interim* Sports Director? The interim part came to an end, and my boss scheduled a meeting with me. It seemed like a formality at that point. I had been doing the job for months, I was working hard, I was getting good feedback, I thought this meeting would be a "congrats and welcome to the team."

It was not.

He told me that there was someone who had applied for the job and they were going to give it to them. This person was coming straight out of college and had already accepted the position.

Let that sink in for a second. It was a feeling I had never felt before, and thankfully haven't since. It felt like all of my energy, all of my feelings, all of my identity just vanished. I was this hollow shell of a person, slumped down in a chair in my boss's office, unable to move. He told me they valued me as an employee, and that I could return to working weekends.

I put in my two weeks' notice the next day.

The Call

To that point, my entire identity had been wrapped up in my work. And that was probably the biggest problem of all. My entire life was defined by my career in the present and the potential of what it would be in the future. It was really all I had thought about for years. From that flyer in my dorm, to the Al Michaels interview, through all the hard work in college, everything was wrapped up in this. I had moved my life to Abilene for...what? It was everything I aspired to be.

And now it was gone.

Think about how you react to failure or huge disappointment. That is an important aspect of your character.

I heard an art teacher at my school tell a story about her summer that moved me to tears.

She spent it in Italy, taking a sculpting class. She was there for weeks, and spent 8-10 hours a day working on her project. She showed us a picture of the complete piece, and it was breathtaking. You could tell she had poured her heart and soul into it.

Once she was done, she meticulously packaged it and shipped it home. She was going to be in Italy for a few days more, but wanted her sculpture to be there waiting for her.

The next photo she showed us was what she found in the package.

When she got home, she opened it to find it full of broken shards.

The audience gasped when we saw the photo. We were devastated for her.

She paused, gathered her breath, and said the most profound words I had ever heard:

"I tell my students all the time that art is a process. That if you think only about the end product, you miss all the steps that lead to the masterpiece. So I don't cry about my lost sculpture. I instead rejoice because I got to be a part of the journey, and that's what matters."

I wish I had heard those words when the news director told me I wasn't good enough. That my dream was impossible, that my whole life before that moment was a sham. Those words would have carried me through a very dark time in my life.

Because that time *was* dark. And it was dark because I fell into what I call the great American trap.

My friend Brad, the used car salesman type, told a story in a sermon he gave about email. He said that when email was being developed, people were hailing it as the savior for the modern workforce. Because of email, we would work 25-hour work weeks like people in Europe. We would have more hobbies, more interests, more time with our families and friends.

America Online, widely regarded as the first mass version of e-mail in America, started in 1985.

That was 36 years ago. Has America slowed down even one bit? Of course it hasn't. And that's not all bad. But e-mail hasn't made our lives simpler at all. It's helped our work lives sneak their way into our personal lives bit by bit over all that time.

So because of this culture of work and go and success and money, I fell into the trap. I became a parts person, instead of a sum person.

I had given an unhealthy amount of importance to the part of my life that was work. I had defined myself really by how well I was doing my job, and where it could take me.

If I had the discernment I have now, I would have been able to see the sum of everything I had gained from my move to Abilene, and realized it was the best thing that could have ever happened to me.

Did my "dream" job fade away? Sure. But think about all the incredible things I had gained from the failure! I got to try out my dream job! I got to taste what that was like!

Most important of all that I gained from the failure was Stephanie, the woman I was in love with. But I also had friends, and memories, and our home, and Bubbles. I had *so* much going for me.

So now it came down to a big decision, and it might be one you have to face someday too. Should I choose my job? Or my life?

Chapter 17
Farewell Rob...See You in 10 Minutes

My last day at the station was my birthday. Steph still tells the story about how silly it was that she was saying this heartfelt goodbye to me on air, and I would still be her ride home.

After a long time feeling sorry for myself, I realized that my journey was only beginning, and the most important part of it had nothing to do with me at all and everything to do with the wonderful human being who I was sharing my life with.

I don't want that choice to sound easy, because it wasn't. I thought a lot about what I really prioritized in life. If you had told me in college, especially after the interview with Al Michaels, that I would ditch my dream for a girl, I would have said you were crazy.

But the crazy part was how I felt about this woman. And whether it's another person, or another career you find, or a life-altering moment, I encourage you to listen to it. The moment or the person might be pointing you to exactly where you need to go.

Steph was from Abilene and had poured her heart into becoming the face of the news station. I let go of the pressure to work my way up to ESPN legend and looked at the life I was building. My priorities had changed. Imagine that. I realized that supporting Steph in her dream was now way more important than the sportscasting gig. Goodbye Bristol, hello Big Country.

Now I had the freedom to reinvent myself. Abilene doesn't have a bustling job market, so it was the only thing I could think to do in town. I enrolled at a local college and got my teaching certificate. I did my student teaching and loved it. Helping young people learn and grow was something I never predicted would impact me in such a profound way.

It took me about 18 months to finish my certificate and student teaching. After that, I started looking for teaching jobs. But before I did that, just for fun, and remembering the chilling ultimatum that Steph had given me about a year and a half earlier, I stopped by the

Pepperdine job board. I looked through the first three pages, and nothing caught my eye.

Then I came to page four.

They had an opening for an Admission Counselor. It was essentially a job where I would travel to places, talk to kids and their families about how awesome Pepperdine was, and help kids get admitted to my favorite college on the planet. And they would even *pay* me to do it!

I submitted an application and then told Steph later that day. I told her it was only a thought, and she was so busy that I don't think she thought much of it.

I got an interview. I dusted off my old sports anchoring suit and interviewed via Skype. I completely nailed it.

And didn't get the job.

I started working at Steph's parents' video stores. There was a Chinese food place next door called Little Panda. I ate there every day. It was magical, probably not for my cholesterol, but still magical.

There was a guy who worked there named Paul. Since I saw him every day, we became friends. He told me that he had made some modifications to his car and invited me to the parking lot to check them out.

The first thing I noticed was a sticker on the back windshield that read, "Hater Vision". Intrigued of course, I asked, "Hey Paul, what does that mean?"

Then he said, "I'll show you."

Paul opened the car, turned on the ignition, hit a switch, and then two monitors flipped up from the back head rests, and immediately started playing a Kanye West music video. The "Hater Vision" sticker made reference to the fact that Paul's haters behind him could see how good he had it in his car. That anyone driving behind him could get a glimpse into his in-car life. Unforgettable.

I was content. A few months later, the job opened up at Pepperdine again. I applied, and they called me. They said that they had an internal candidate, and they were going to give them the job.

About a year later it opened again. I applied as an afterthought because I never expected it to work. But third time's the charm. They offered the job to me, and I said I needed to talk to my wife, the television star.

I mean, really, she was. They even put her on the side of a city bus. My family had a field day with that.

Steph had every right to say I was nuts. Why would she leave her dream career for this? We had this lovely little life in her hometown, and I was trying to uproot her to California?

I told her I wasn't going to take it. And that we would live in Abilene for as long as she wanted. It made the most sense.

Luckily for me, and for this story, Stephanie Rose Mooring doesn't give a damn about what makes sense.

She said we had to do it. She said it was our next adventure, and that if we didn't take this chance now, while we were young and childless, then we never would. And if we didn't, we wouldn't be able to live with ourselves.

Again, I get it. I have no idea why she is married to me either.

So we packed up our house and moved to Santa Monica. Because I am a genius, I figured Steph's car had a trailer hitch, so we would just rent a U-Haul. On the evening before the move, I realized there was no trailer hitch. We called our friend Derrick, who was good at getting us out of jams. He came over to help. Our car turned out like this:

We drove over 1,200 miles like that. We moved in with one of my buddies from elementary school named Sam.

I started my job, and loved it. Steph became a full-time nanny, and loved it. Living in Santa Monica did turn out to be a wonderful adventure. We spent about two years there.

While working in admissions at Pepperdine, I started to realize how many people along the way had made sure I had made it to this life that I was loving. My mom and my sisters encouraged me to take risks and get an education. My friends that I left when I went to college were my cheerleaders, thousands of miles away. And my friends in college, were my support network, even when my parents' relationship was dissolving. All of them had a major role in getting me to Pepperdine, and thus, to this life I had now.

And now, I got to do the same for kids. My privilege had come full circle, so it was time for me to pay it forward.

Matt's Short Résumé

A colleague and I started a program called the Pepperdine Summer Preview, or PSP. We wanted to create a bridge program for low-income, first-generation college students to get acclimated to campus life. We had a student decide not to attend Pepperdine the year before because they were scared to make the transition from home to college, and it rocked us to our core. So we set up this program to help as many kids as we could, but one maybe more so in particular.

One day when we were reading applications as a committee, we ran across a student named Matt. He was a stellar kid. He took really difficult classes and had awesome test scores. Then we looked at his résumé, and it had one entry.

We were stunned. Usually kids like Matt were involved in *everything* because they were such overachievers. But thankfully we looked a little deeper.

His lone résumé entry was working for Pizza Hut as an Area Hiring Manager. I didn't know what that really meant, so I called his college counselor at his high school to find out. She told me the most devastating and inspirational story I had ever heard.

She said that Matt's father was dead and that his mother was an addict. His Mother and Stepfather were abusive to him and his half-brother, so much so that Matt was scared to leave him to go away for college. Matt told me stories about how his parents would forbid him from talking unless spoken to, and if he did, he would face serious consequences. He said he would pass the time by thinking about things he didn't know. His brilliant intellect was the only silver lining in that dark cloud of abuse.

Neither of his parents worked, so in order to *feed* his family, Matt got a job cleaning houses at his apartment complex when he was 12. He got paid under the table.

At 14, he got a job working with a house flipper on home remodeling projects and kept getting paid under the table.

On his literal 16th birthday, Matt got an application to work at Pizza Hut.

It took Pizza Hut all of four months to realize that they had a unicorn working for them, so they trained him to become Restaurant General Manager. By the end of the year, they promoted him to Area Hiring Manager. He was seventeen years old and in charge of hiring, training, and firing people.

When he turned eighteen, they gave him another promotion, and told him that if he stayed, they would eventually make him the GM of the store. He would have made sixty-five thousand dollars at age 18.

And Matt said no.

How does a kid coming from that home life say no? The fact that he saw college as a way to not only give him financial stability, but a career he actually loved, is nothing short of heroic. He had every right to stay, but thankfully he had the foresight to leave. He said it was especially hard because he was supporting his entire family, and his Mom begged him on her hands and knees to stay.

And he didn't achieve the incredible things at Pizza Hut to boost his résumé to hopefully get into college. He did it because he *had* to. He did it to help his family survive.

His counselor told me that she was worried Matt wouldn't come to Pepperdine because of his family situation, and also because he didn't have anything to bring to college with him. I called my sisters, told them the story, and they said, "Get a list. We will take care of it."

We were expecting the list to have things like sheets, maybe a computer, some bookshelves, you know, what most kids take with them to college.

Here was the entire list:

Toothpaste
Shampoo
Deodorant
A New Toothbrush
Socks
Shoes
Pants
Shirts

I was never poor like Matt was, but I knew what it was like to live in fear. As many days as I could, I would go to my friends' houses after school to stay away from my house. Because invariably, I would walk into an argument, or something being thrown or broken.

There were so many fights, but one I remember vividly was my dad breaking at least 10-15 dishes in our kitchen. I hid in my room until it was over and went to the kitchen to help my mom clean up the mess. I asked her what it was about this time, and she said, calmly and almost lifelessly, "They said he couldn't be a little league coach".

Matt's story resonated with me in so many ways, but more than anything, Matt inspired me to be a better person. His courage changed how I looked at the world.

Not surprisingly, Matt graduated from Pepperdine in three years. A year early. He then was accepted to law schools across the country, but Pepperdine gave him a full-tuition scholarship. He took it.

Matt now is a big-time lawyer in LA and makes six figures. Not bad for a pizza boy.

Working with Matt was the joy of my life. But I knew there were more Matts out there.

Buns and Ovens and Plans

It didn't take long for Steph's biological clock to start ticking, so we tried to start a family. It was early on in the process. We went to the local CVS to pick up some feminine products, and Steph threw in a pregnancy test just for fun. You should have seen the look on the poor cashier's face. He looked at the pads, and the pregnancy test, and then back at me. Not one to miss an opportunity for an awkward encounter, I said, "Welp. It's one or the other!"

It was the other. Steph was pregnant with a baby girl. We were ecstatic. And then I got terrified.

I knew Steph wanted to be a stay-at-home mom. I also knew that we couldn't afford to live on a single income in Santa Monica. I was having an existential crisis one night. It was 11 PM, and I was the only one awake. I borrowed Sam's computer and googled, "College Guidance Counselor Houston Texas." I figured that my experience at Pepperdine would qualify me for that job. If we lived in Houston, we'd be close to my family and somewhat close to hers. And we could probably live on one income.

The first web link that popped up changed my life forever.

It was for a high school called YES Prep.

I didn't know a lot about YES Prep, but I saw on their website that they worked with under-resourced students in the Houston area. The school went to the poorest and toughest neighborhoods, hoping to provide an education and college counseling model that rivaled more affluent districts.

It was a no-brainer for me to apply. It seemed like a school *full* of kids like Matt.

They asked me on the application which campus I wanted to work at. Now I had grown a lot from the aimless idiot I was in high school, but I was in no way a finished product.

A normal, sensible person might have looked up where the

campuses were, figured out how close they were to places where we might live, and then go from there.

Nope. I marked the big button that read, "No Preference."

Well done.

A few weeks later, I had a phone interview. A few weeks after that, they invited me to interview at their East End campus. I had no idea where that was, but I bought a plane ticket, and flew down and stayed with my Mom the night before the interview.

Whenever I have a job interview, I leave super early. This one especially, because there was this kid I would need to start feeding in 4-5 months. As I was driving to campus, a feeling of familiarity hit me.

My mom and dad grew up in the East End of Houston. My Great Aunt lived in a tiny house in the area with no air conditioning. We would spend summer days at her house, trying to survive the heat, and she would make us fried chicken in a cast iron skillet.

Sometimes, when it's really hot, my sisters and I joke that we can still smell that chicken.

As I drove to YES Prep for my interview, I pulled down a familiar street.

It was my Great Aunt's. I passed where her old house was on my way.

I figured if they offered me the job, that was probably a pretty good sign to take it. They did. And it was.

Toy Cash Registers and Perspective

Our daughter Molly was born on June 12, 2012. We moved back to Houston, and I started at YES Prep on July 9th.

Working at YES Prep changed my view on everything. From

124

politics, to education, to equity, to social justice, my entire worldview was flipped upside down. I owe so much of who I am to the experience, and if I was 22 and single, I would still be there.

But I am clearly not. I fell in love so deeply with my work at YES Prep that they got the best version of me. Molly and Steph got the leftovers. Finding a job you are passionate about can be a double-edged sword. It feels good to give your energy to an endeavor that is deeply meaningful and allows you to help others in a life-changing way. At the same time, that sometimes comes at the expense of a work-life balance.

I had to make a decision to be the best father and husband I could be. It was the hardest decision of my life, but for the sake of being more present with my family, I took a new job at another school in Houston. I was lucky to find a place like St. Agnes. They took a chance on me, and I will always admire and appreciate them for that. This job has given me the perfect combination of work-life balance and ability to help kids pursue their dreams in life. I have been here six years, and I have never been afflicted with the "Sunday Scaries." Every Monday I am rejuvenated and refreshed by the work, the place where I work, and the people I work with. I consider myself to be one lucky son of a gun.

Luckiest of all, I am a dad. Molly is the best person I know. I want to be like her when I grow up. The problem with having a kid like Molly is that you get overly confident as a parent. Arrogant is not too strong of a word. We thought to ourselves, "This parenting thing is a piece of cake. Let's do the world a favor and bring more light into it." So we did. And we got this guy:

Owen Mooring was born on January 6th, 2016, and he has really had that face on the entire time. But he is hilarious, so we haven't put him up for adoption yet.

And even with all of this, life isn't perfect.

The Call

A while back, the Moorings had a bank account balance of $8.27. That $8.27 represented the entirety of the liquid assets of me, my wife, and my two young children, and both of those freeloaders are currently unemployed.

It was also six days until payday.

Our fridge looked like our house had been inhabited by a degenerate bachelor. Stephanie, the aforementioned saint of a woman who married a recovering, degenerate bachelor, had an idea.

"Hey, I've got a bunch of change in a Ziploc bag! We can use it for groceries."

She pulled out a plastic bag full of coins, probably no more than 20 bucks. Enough to probably get us through the week. We aren't poor. We don't drive fancy cars, or get invited to yacht parties, but we get by. So the grocery problem was solved. I went back to washing dishes. Then my four-year-old daughter saw the bag of change sitting on the table. Here she is a little older:

"WHOA!!!! That is a LOT of money. That's the most money I've seen in my whole life!"

I said supportively, yet condescendingly, "That is a lot of money, kiddo." And then I went back to washing dishes again.

I heard some commotion behind me, so I turned around, and Molly had three shiny pennies in her hand. She took them from her toy cash register, and was putting them in the bag.

"What are you doing, Molly?"

"Well, these are money, too. For groceries!"

It was like getting hit with a ton of bricks.

It's hard keeping up with the Joneses. It's tough to see people with nicer cars than you, or to see pictures on Instagram of people on exotic vacations. Whether you are a single-income family, or a no-income family, or a kid trying to keep up with your peers, it's challenging to have a healthy sense of self-worth. But that kid and those three pennies gave me a profound realization. None of that garbage matters.

If we were rich, I wouldn't be typing these words. I wouldn't have had the opportunity to see a four-year-old, with clearly more perspective than most adults I know, including myself, giving me the secret to life. Those three pennies represented much more than a contribution to the stuff in our grocery cart. It was proof positive that your success, your happiness, your self-concept, has everything to do with your attitude, and not how much money you have in your bank account.

It is incredible how life experience changes your perceptions of what is important. And there's no way to get the experience other than to live, one day at a time. I think back to the person I was in high school and college. I'd never have imagined my current life in a million years. But I love it. So go after what you want. Believe in yourself. Chase the impossible. But don't forget what's really important. Work hard and be kind.

I went after my dream, and I failed. I didn't make it. But guess what? This *incredible* life that I live now *never* would have happened if I had succeeded. And I can't imagine a better life than I have now.

Chapter 18
Soooooo, Now What?

You've done it. You made it to the end of the story. But what now?

You probably won't work at a local TV station in West Texas, or play chess with your ex-con neighbor, and hopefully won't store your suits on the floor of an apartment with no air conditioning.

My story has had a ton of twists and turns, but no matter where you are, or where you are going, I hope my story has resonated with you in some way.

Remember the questions that I mentioned at the beginning of the book?

How do I make sure I get into the right college and choose the right major?

What am I going to do with my life?

What if I want something different than my family and teachers expect?

My biggest hope for you, after reading my story, is that you know it's okay to not know. The not knowing part is where growth and change happen.

And whether you are young or old, it's okay to not know what you want to do with your life. I am getting really old, and I still have no idea. I tell my students that I love what I am doing *right now*. And guess what? I have said that about every other job I have ever had. And then things happen that change my idea about what I want to do or where I want to do it, so I try new things. And when you try new things, you either like the new thing, or you don't, but regardless, learning and growth are happening. You are figuring out which parts of your life truly matter.

And knowing the answer is *not* as important as trusting your gut, failing with grace and positivity, and keeping your eyes open to new possibilities, not only in your job, but in the people that surround you in your life.

The Call

So go. Make a plan, but don't chain yourself to it. Allow yourself to grow, change, learn, and love. Cherish your relationships, believe in yourself, and go after what you want.

I watch the Oscars every year with my family because we like to guess and keep track of who does the best. The 2014 Oscars was about the same as every other Oscar night.

But then Matthew McConaughey won an Oscar.

What he said I am sure no one in the world saw coming. His speech was brilliant, but this part stuck out to me the most:

> *Now when I was 15 years old, I had a very important person in my life come to me and say, "Who is your hero?" And I said I don't know I gotta think about that, give me a couple of weeks. I come back two weeks later, this person comes up and says "Who's your hero?" And so I thought about it and I said you know who it is, it's me in 10 years...*

> *...So you see every day, every week, every month and every year of my life, my hero is always 10 years away. I'm never going to beat my hero. I'm not going to obtain that, I know I'm not. And that's just fine with me because that keeps me with somebody to keep on chasing.*

If you spend your life chasing others, or chasing money, you might get there, but the journey usually isn't fun, and the end isn't always peachy either.

But if you chase the best version of yourself and take moments to appreciate the journey, then it could lead you to a life you didn't know was possible.

I went from a local TV star (or at least being married to one), to a nine-to-five desk jockey, and I couldn't be happier.

So go! Go after what you want. You deserve it. And I'm pulling for you.

Made in the USA
Columbia, SC
11 June 2024